REPAIRING THE DAMAGE
Possibilities and limits of transatlantic consensus

DANA H. ALLIN, GILLES ANDRÉANI,
PHILIPPE ERRERA AND GARY SAMORE

ADELPHI PAPER 389

The International Institute for Strategic Studies

Arundel House ┃ 13–15 Arundel Street ┃ Temple Place ┃ London ┃ WC2R 3DX ┃ UK

ADELPHI PAPER 389

First published August 2007 by **Routledge**
4 Park Square, Milton Park, Abingdon, Oxon, OX14 4RN

for **The International Institute for Strategic Studies**
Arundel House, 13–15 Arundel Street, Temple Place, London, WC2R 3DX, UK
www.iiss.org

Simultaneously published in the USA and Canada by **Routledge**
270 Madison Ave., New York, NY 10016

Routledge is an imprint of Taylor & Francis, an Informa Business

© 2007 The International Institute for Strategic Studies

DIRECTOR-GENERAL AND CHIEF EXECUTIVE John Chipman
EDITOR Patrick Cronin
MANAGER FOR EDITORIAL SERVICES Ayse Abdullah
ASSISTANT EDITOR Katharine Fletcher
PRODUCTION John Buck
COVER IMAGES Getty Images

Printed and bound in Great Britain by Bell & Bain Ltd, Thornliebank, Glasgow

British Library Cataloguing in Publication Data
A catalogue record for this book is available from the British Library

Library of Congress Cataloging in Publication Data

ISBN 978-0-415-41869-0
ISSN 0567-932X

Contents

GLOSSARY

CBMs	confidence-building measures
BWC	Biological Weapons Convention
DRC	Democratic Republic of the Congo
E3	UK, France and Germany (in relation to negotiations on Iran's nuclear programme)
E3+3	E3 plus Russia, US and China
IAEA	International Atomic Energy Agency
ISAF	International Security Assistance Force
ISI	Inter-Services Intelligence
KEDO	Korean Peninsula Energy Development Organisation
NPT	Nuclear Non-Proliferation Treaty
NSG	Nuclear Suppliers' Group
PA	Palestinian Authority
PSI	Proliferation Security Initiative
P5	United Nations Security Council Permanent 5
UF$_6$	uranium hexafluoride
UNIFIL 2	United Nations Interim Force in Lebanon (from 2006)
UNMOVIC	United Nations Monitoring, Verification and Inspection Commission
UNSCR	United Nations Security Council Resolution
WMD	weapons of mass destruction

This Adelphi Paper benefited from the advice and help of many people. The IISS transatlantic steering group and other participants contributed to a series of stimulating workshops. For their input into successive drafts we would particularly like to thank Patrick Cronin, Toby Dodge, Mark Fitzpatrick, Katharine Fletcher, Tim Huxley, Yumi Kim, Christopher Langton, Jeffrey Mazo, Ben Rhode, Friedrich Schroeder, Steven N. Simon, Walter Slocombe and Marina Vaughan. The paper is stronger because of their help; weaknesses and errors are the authors' own.

Ten Propositions for Transatlantic Consensus

Alliances are normally formed to serve a specific purpose, an agenda. In history, alliances tended to be temporary, tightly conditional, and limited to a specific task, the *casus foederis* of traditional diplomatic parlance. Once that task was accomplished, they normally dissolved, or gave way to a new alliance better suited to the new problems at hand.

The winning allies in the Second World War emerged from that conflict with a more ambitious idea: to embed their alliance permanently in the fabric of a new international order of peace, prosperity and law. This ambition to convert coalition sword into United Nations ploughshare is reflected today in the continuing permanent membership of the UN Security Council. Of course, the rapid break-up of that coalition into opposing Cold War blocs confirmed the proposition that no alliance is eternal. Yet the Atlantic alliance carried something of the same ambition, and when the Cold War ended, the assumption survived that this alliance would remain as an important bulwark of a structured 'international community'.

This ambition demanded that the Atlantic alliance establish its continued relevance, which required finding a plausible agenda both for consolidating an essentially favourable status quo, and grappling with new challenges. It found one in the 1990s: 'expanding stability in Europe', through enlargement and through re-establishing order in the Balkans. This twin agenda is now mostly behind us. Enlargement is approaching its natural limit, while the uneasy peace in the Balkans will have to be secured more through the efforts of the European Union than the broader alliance.

It was in this context that the transatlantic partnership entered a new century and encountered three new sources of stress. Firstly, a new US administration presented a sharply nationalist aversion to multilateral treaties; rejecting the Kyoto Protocol on climate change, withdrawing from the treaty establishing an International Criminal Court and scuppering the proposed compliance protocol to the Biological Weapons Convention (BWC). Following the US Senate's 1999 rejection of the Comprehensive Test Ban Treaty, these moves deepened a sense of transatlantic mutual alienation over international norms. To be sure, this Jacksonian view of American interests had achieved political dominance by the narrowest of margins in a most controversial election, and it could certainly be argued that a majority of the American electorate remained closer to the traditional transatlantic consensus.[1] Nonetheless, the White House's robust combination of neo-conservative idealism and Jacksonian assertions of national sovereignty certainly strained that consensus.

The second source of stress was the catastrophic terrorism inflicted upon the Twin Towers in New York, the Pentagon in Washington and in the air over Pennsylvania. This crisis could have provided – and indeed might yet provide – a new strategic focus for the alliance. The day after the attacks, America's allies invoked, for the first and only time, Article 5 of their mutual defence treaty, which states that an attack on one member is an attack on all; and from this invocation has flowed the ongoing NATO effort at nation-building in Afghanistan. Yet, for all the solidarity engendered by the trauma of 11 September, there were bound to be serious problems with shifting the allies' strategic focus from Europe, where they generally agreed, to the Middle East, where they found agreement more difficult.

The third stress, the invasion of Iraq, led to genuine crisis and arguably posed an existential threat to the alliance. This was not, certainly, because the disagreement about the war was based on inherent, irreconcilable differences over terrorism, or war and peace. In Afghanistan European governments and publics had readily supported a war to topple a regime that was not directly responsible for 11 September. On the American side, according to US opinion polls, as of late 2005 a majority of Americans had concluded that the invasion and occupation of Iraq had been a counter-strategic diversion and complication in the struggle against terrorism – in effect, a self-inflicted wound. It is difficult, therefore, to support the notion that the Iraq disagreement somehow reflected a fundamental strategic divergence between Americans and continental Europeans.

The invasion of Iraq and the subsequent ongoing conflict there did, however, place an extra burden on attempts to reconstitute a robust transatlantic partnership. It could be seen in 2005 as both Americans and Europeans sought to repair their relationship. Ideological acrimony had subsided into a mood of businesslike, if sometimes sullen, accommodation. Substantive cooperation, which in truth never stopped, has been aided by this shift in mood. Paris and Washington worked together closely at the UN to fashion a resolution that preceded Syria's withdrawal from Lebanon. Meanwhile, the Bush administration and key European governments were finally able to craft compatible, if not quite congruent, policies for confronting Iran's nuclear ambitions.

The problem for both sides, however, is that they were coming back together at a time of palpable mutual weakness. While this ensures that each needs the other, it also underscores the limits of what they can accomplish, even if united.

The alliance now needs to define its post-11 September and post-Iraq agenda. That agenda will have to be a selective one – more eclectic, flexible and subject to change than before. For the alliance to survive, much less thrive, in this new and more demanding context, two conditions will have to be met. First, Europe and the United States will have to develop compatible strategic frameworks within which to operate and, more importantly, select the issues for which their new à la carte alliance can be of relevance. A corollary is that they should learn how not to agree, and even strongly disagree, on those issues on which they have chosen not to act jointly. Despite the significant conceptual divergences of the last three years, the strategic frameworks of Europe and the US need not be irreconcilable. Properly managed, the differences could be turned into a beneficial complementarity, once the main points of contention have been overcome.

In some respects this points towards a more modest definition of the alliance's remit. The partnership will be a limited one insofar as there will inevitably be major challenges, such as posed by the rise of China, where transatlantic disparities in strategic means and commitments will mainly preclude any common alliance undertaking. Yet such limits, and considerable divergences of policies and inclinations, are nothing new. The absence of a common transatlantic commitment to counter-insurgency in Iraq may cause resentments, but so too did the lack of a common commitment to counter-insurgency in Vietnam.

In other respects, there is a transatlantic security agenda that remains quite ambitious. In this paper we suggest ten propositions for future transatlantic consensus on security challenges for which the allies should be able to agree on common approaches. These are:

1. **Reaffirmation by the transatlantic partners that human rights, rule of law and democracy are intrinsic to the Atlantic relationship as an alliance of democratic nations.** This requires, as first priority, the unambiguous recommitment to the humane treatment of captured combatants and terrorist suspects, the prohibition of torture and other forms of mistreatment, and access of detainees to due process of judgment and law. Without this recommitment, the credibility of the alliance's human rights and democracy agenda will be very difficult to restore. Although the transatlantic partners will not be able to agree on the urgency of radical democratic change in the Middle East, they can and should coalesce around a global commitment to human rights and more gradual democratic reform.

2. **Transatlantic leadership in reinforcing the prohibition on state support for terrorism, and promoting further Security Council-sponsored rules to address such issues as the illicit transfer of weapons of mass destruction (WMD) and their components.** The aim should be to establish the clearest presumption that manifest state support for terrorism, or violation of various prohibitions against WMD possession or use, could entail international sanctions and possibly military action. Such presumptions go hand-in-hand with developing concepts of humanitarian law: the 'responsibility to protect' against near-genocidal violations of human rights, and the prospect of intervention in states that cannot or will not prevent their territories from becoming bases for international terrorism, suggest new limits to traditional notions of state sovereignty.

3. **A concerted strategy to prevent Iran from developing a nuclear-weapons capability.** Achieving the full and verified suspension of all Iranian nuclear fuel cycle related activities and the satisfaction of the demands of the International Atomic Energy Agency (IAEA) requires ongoing effective coordination in multilateral forums, as well as continued bilateral efforts to engage countries such as Russia, China and India. The vital medium-term goal of rolling back illicit Iranian nuclear activities also requires a longer-term effort on the part of the European Union and the United States to redefine the region's security equation.

4. **A broader strategy to strengthen the non-proliferation regime and to mitigate the threat of catastrophic terrorism.** Such a strategy would include making an agreement to limit the spread of sensitive fuel-cycle technologies, finding a way to deal more resolutely with states in non-compliance with their non-proliferation commitments – in particular those who wish to withdraw from the Nuclear Non-Proliferation Treaty (NPT) – and strengthening the powers of the IAEA. To combat the risk of catastrophic terrorism, these actions need to be complemented by a major upgrade of current efforts to secure nuclear, chemical and biological materials and by enhanced efforts, using the Proliferation Security Initiative (PSI), to stop illicit trade in nuclear, biological and chemical weapons technology. Europeans and Americans can play a key role in reinforcing the BWC, and in enforcing the Chemical Weapons Convention, in particular its provisions on challenge inspections. There should also be a transatlantic commitment to a fully funded system for reducing the related threats posed by biological terrorism and natural global pandemics. This commitment entails a recognition that the first line of defence against both avian flu and terrorist-engineered smallpox, for instance, would be a robust globally integrated set of public health systems.

5. **A US and EU undertaking to promote the establishment of a regional security forum for the Middle East, with the first goal of facilitating Iraq's integration into regional arrangements, thus committing Iraq's neighbours to the country's stabilisation.** At a later point, the forum should be broadened to encompass other key regional security issues, such as terrorism and proliferation, drawing on the precedent of the Arms Control and Regional Security effort of the Madrid Process after the 1991 Gulf War.

6. **Concerted transatlantic diplomacy focused on the minimal goal of keeping open the option of an Israel–Palestine peace based on a two-state solution.** In the short run, and notwithstanding the January 2006 Hamas election victory, neither the Europeans nor the Americans can afford to allow the territories under Palestinian authority to fall into deprivation and chaos. In the longer run, there will have to be a renewed commitment to a negotiated two-state solution, probably requiring a joint Euro-American statement of the parameters that are necessary for any such solution to be viable.

7. **A joint undertaking to support the United Nations as peace-keeper and state-builder 'of first resort' in the nations and regions afflicted by state failure.** The deployment, successful so far, of European forces in the UN's UNIFIL 2 mission in southern Lebanon is one of many reminders that UN peacekeeping operations remain an indispensable vehicle for conflict resolution. It also shows that it was a mistake for both the Europeans and Americans to effectively desert UN peacekeeping operations, and subcontract global peace-keeping to Third World or post-Soviet armies, over the preceding decade. Where they did intervene themselves in that period – for example, the UK in Sierra Leone, France in Côte d'Ivoire, the EU in the Democratic Republic of the Congo (DRC) – Europeans and Americans remained formally outside the UN operation. This kind of separation is damaging to the UN's principles of equality and universality.

8. **A transatlantic undertaking to train and equip NATO and EU forces, *as a matter of priority*, for their most likely missions – comprehensive peacekeeping and stabilisation missions,** with the recognition that success or failure of the enterprise in Afghanistan is likely to be the single most important test for NATO as such over the remaining years of this decade.

9. **A determination to coordinate NATO and EU military operations on the basis of strategic rather than bureaucratic considerations.** Petty competition needs to be curtailed. Substantive considerations such as risk (who is committing troops on the ground) and politi-cal initiative (who proposed intervention in the first place) should have precedence. The US should not hesitate to support 'pure' EU operations, if the centre of gravity of those operations is clearly European. Likewise EU members should not indulge in arguments over whose flag an operation should be under, especially in cases where no one is ready to intervene.

10. **Effective transatlantic leadership for international cooperation to reduce carbon emissions and fight global warming.** Impending catastrophic climate change may turn out to be the greatest secu-rity threat that the world faces, and it is a threat that cannot be addressed without united action by the world's richest democra-cies. Every security threat of the post-modern era – the grievances

that stoke terrorism, nuclear proliferation by fragile or failing states, massive refugee flows and fights over territory evolving to ethnic cleansing or even genocide – will be aggravated immeasurably by any dramatic reduction in the carrying capacity of this densely populated planet. It follows ineluctably that curtailment of carbon emissions is the *sine qua non* of every other effort to shape and preserve a peaceful international order.

If pursued with seriousness and a reasonable degree of transatlantic unity, these propositions could constitute the foundations of an effective working partnership. They are, in our view, the basis for consensus on the most pressing security challenges that the allies face. They are daunting, certainly, but also limited, in the sense that agreement on most of these propositions would not require full agreement on broader principles of international order. It would not be necessary, for example, for Washington and Paris to have the same view of the authority of the Security Council to regulate the use of force, of national sovereignty vs global norms, of the International Criminal Court, etc. It is a pragmatic, ad hoc list of propositions, not an architecture for world order.

It is also the case that each of these propositions might be interpreted at such a level of banality as to render them meaningless in terms of bolstering common transatlantic policies. As we set out these propositions as areas of common strategic ground in more detail, we also discuss the limits of consensus. Our lodestar is realism about the alliance and the world as it is, not as we wish it to be.

One requirement of realism in this context is to concede that there will be security problems on which transatlantic unity might be urgently needed, but is currently unavailable. Common action against global warming might be seen to be such a problem: at least until the Democrats' victory in November 2006 House and Senate elections, there was no indication that either the US executive or Congress was willing to take *any* steps to conserve energy or lower carbon emissions.

We nonetheless felt constrained to put the issue on our list. The scientific consensus has solidified: the time frame for taking action against this potential catastrophe is something like ten years: in other words, shorter than any reasonable estimate of the time it might take to win a hearts and minds campaign to tame the anger of millions of Muslims who are susceptible to the claims of radical and violent Islamism. The time frame for experiencing catastrophic climate change could be something in the order of 50 years: in other words, the prospect that millions could be uprooted or killed by the consequences of global warming is as imminent and at least as plausible as the prospect that terrorists might kill tens or hundreds of thousands with nuclear or biological weapons. Put another way, the children of the authors of this paper can expect to grow to middle age in a world that is shaped – politically and morally as well as ecologically – by this planetary crisis.

The inability or unwillingness of the planet's two biggest carbon polluters, China and the US, to restrain themselves is daunting. But against this political inertia and, in China's case, an overriding imperative to economic growth, there are two encouraging factors. Firstly, the measures to cope with the problem are technically and economically feasible.[2] Carbon emission, as American writer Gregg Easterbrook reminds us, is an air pollution problem, and since the 1970s air pollution problems have been tackled more effectively and more cheaply than almost anyone expected they could be.[3] Secondly, the urgency with which Britain – the most Atlanticist of the major European powers – has seized on this issue suggests at least a reasonable chance of extending the consensus across the Atlantic. In any event, continued inability on the part of the world's leading democracies to cooperate against potentially catastrophic climate change could hardly be considered a sign of an effective transatlantic partnership. Solving this problem will require international cooperation on a level that will constitute a quantum change in global governance comparable to the establishment of the Bretton Woods institutions of the immediate post-war era.[4] It is beyond the scope of this essay, but the renewed habit of transatlantic cooperation posited here would be a precondition for meeting such a challenge.

There are other transatlantic divergences that can be partially bridged. It will be necessary, but also difficult, to combine continued transatlantic cooperation on direct counter-terrorism with a serious dialogue on how to move beyond the concept of a 'war on terrorism' to address the wider problem and causes of Islamist extremism. It is not clear that even a future US administration will be willing or able to abandon or de-emphasise the 'long war' as a key organising theme of American foreign policy. But it seems increasingly the case that the concept of war, which could be discounted in the early months after 11 September as a matter of semantics, is itself a polarising factor in transatlantic relations. This important conceptual disagreement is taken up in Chapter One.

Ironically, the transatlantic alliance also lacks a common position on Russia. There has been a careless assumption that the peaceful end of the Cold War rendered consensus on what had been the alliance's primary focus irrelevant. But the relevance is returning. The alliance needs to react to more assertive Russian policies across a range of issues, including energy supply, Kosovo, missile defence, and Moscow's threat to withdraw from the Conventional Armed Forces in Europe Treaty. There will be increasing pressures to develop a more coordinated strategy; hasty and inadequately examined ideas – such as Ukrainian or Georgian membership of NATO – do not appear to us to suggest a coherent understanding of this problem.

Finally, there is a need to develop minimal codes of conduct for accommodating the rise of emerging powers such as China, India and Brazil. These codes would be far more modest than common strategies, which are probably beyond reach. But they would probably entail more effective transatlantic consultation on such matters as the EU's bid to lift its arms embargo on China, or the American agreement to normalise nuclear relations with India.

*   *   *

This paper grew out of a series of workshops that began in June 2004, in which the IISS convened a core steering group along with a group of other experts to discuss the crisis in transatlantic relations. Leading themes included the challenges of proliferation and state failure, which of course were central to the discussions of Iraq, the proximate cause of the transatlantic crisis. The participation of steering group members is gratefully acknowledged at the end of this paper, but the views expressed are solely those of the authors.

The authors are two Americans and two Frenchmen. We did not consciously seek a drafting committee composed of citizens of the two most polarised protagonists of the Iraq dispute, but the composition of the team may be, nonetheless, appropriate. The French–American difficulties of recent years, in many ways a reflection of broader transatlantic difficulties, have clearly been harmful for both countries and for the transatlantic alliance.

For France, to be perceived as structurally opposed to the United States has not been good for its influence in Europe and is not consonant with its interests as a Western, developed and democratic nation. The practice of trying to insulate ongoing constructive military and counter-terrorist cooperation, along with equally good cooperation on specific areas of diplomacy, such as Lebanon, from generally troubled political relations, is schizophrenic and perhaps unsustainable. France and the United States share important values and interests, and should be more ready to publicise this reality.

For the United States, it has been a convenient but deeply deceptive fiction to imagine or pretend that disagreements with Europe were a matter of endemic French dissent, rather than genuine and broader transatlantic differences. France does not only speak for itself. It has articulated much wider European perceptions of US policies, and an aspiration to more equal European–US relations that is by no means confined to Paris. It is true that the US and France stand at opposite ends of the spectrum of transatlantic attitudes; but by the same token, repairing French–US relations is the most decisive, if not the easiest, way of repairing transatlantic relations.

France needs to devote more time and energy to the transatlantic link as a positive part of its diplomatic agenda, rather than treating the alliance as a constraint, or something to be taken for granted. The United States needs to understand that for all of France's current difficulties – for example, the rejection by its electorate of the EU Constitutional Treaty – Paris will remain a pivotal leader in the European Union.

Spring 2007 elections in France installed a president and a foreign minister with no qualms about openly supporting Washington when French and American interests and policies are compatible. Some 18 months earlier, the German chancellor's office was assumed by a woman who was unencumbered by her predecessor's bitter personal relationship with the American president. President Bush leaves office at the beginning of 2009. Britain has a new prime minister. It would be facile to suggest that tensions in transatlantic relations will vanish with the changing of the guard. It is possible, however, that new leaders both in the US and throughout Europe will be better able to put the disputes of the recent past behind them. This essay is a guide to the possibilities, and the limits, of a new start.

CHAPTER ONE

Beyond the War on Terror

The Western alliance of the Cold War had its own disagreements, but it also had clarity of purpose. It was intended to address one problem, the Soviet threat in Europe. It did so within the conceptual framework of a defensive military strategy, coupled – over the decades – with détente and political engagement with the Soviet Union. There was also clarity as to where the alliance ended, and a tacit agreement to tolerate disagreements on many issues not covered by the North Atlantic Treaty: in the Middle East regarding the Suez crisis, the various Arab–Israeli wars and the OPEC oil embargo; in Asia regarding Vietnam and China.

These clear boundaries and purpose are gone. The present security agenda is a daunting one that includes the struggle against Islamist terrorism, strategies against nuclear proliferation, and the stabilisation of failed or failing states. All of these concerns affect Americans and Europeans alike, but this does not mean that they can provide the same degree of strategic focus as was supplied by the Soviet adversary. In particular – and notwithstanding its central place in American politics and among the allies' threat perceptions – the fight against terrorism will not provide the alliance with a new, overarching purpose to substitute for its Cold War missions.

This is not to suggest that there are any inevitable disagreements of substance dividing Europe from the United States when it comes to fighting terrorism. The 11 September attacks galvanised genuine Western unity, among both publics and governments. Since 2001, every Western democracy has consistently identified global terrorism as its most pressing security concern, along with the proliferation of WMD. The same judgement has been expressed collectively within the European Union and NATO. Practical cooperation has been intense and effective.[1]

But the conceptual elevation of counter-terrorism to a 'global war on terrorism' is highly problematic, and it is not something that the transatlantic partners can share in. In part this is because the US administration's association of the Iraq War with this global 'war' has compromised the latter in the eyes of many Europeans. Yet, even as acrimony over the Iraq War subsides, and even as new governments and administrations in key alliance capitals settle in, with opportunities to start afresh and renew transatlantic ties, the concept of a war on terrorism is likely to remain more alienating than inspiring for the alliance.

The concept is polarising rather than unifying for three broad reasons. Firstly, the tactics that the United States has used in prosecuting this 'war' have tended to accentuate the overweening aspects of US power and its perceived disregard for international law and global norms. The Bush administration's argument that torture of detainees at Abu Ghraib was a matter of isolated behaviour by out-of-control enlisted personnel has failed to convince its global audience; and indeed, the Pentagon's own investigating commission concluded that the abusive 'interrogation techniques' used at Abu Ghraib and elsewhere had 'migrated', having been debated at the highest levels of the White House, Pentagon and State Department, and approved for use on terrorist suspects at Guantanamo Bay.[2]

Secondly, whereas America's terrorism problem is mainly external, for others the problem is largely internal, and is one of infectious ideology more than hardened enemies. It is not possible for America's European allies to declare 'war' on a sizeable element in their own large Muslim minorities.[3]

Thirdly, the overwhelming preoccupation with terrorism that is implied by mobilisation for war seems out of proportion to Europeans and many others. Terrorism is nowhere near the top of the list of concerns for most of the world. This is not a matter of blind complacency; other threats and worries do in fact loom larger. American solipsism on this score is understandable, to be sure. The large loss of life on 11 September and the powerful horrific theatre of those attacks had a profound effect on American perceptions of the world. Americans intuited, correctly, that a line had been crossed by terrorists who now harboured genocidal – rather than only strategic and political – ambitions. If al-Qaeda or its imitators acquire and master the use of nuclear or biological weapons, then the ambition to kill not thousands, but hundreds of thousands or even millions, could be realisable. Europeans would be likely targets as well as Americans; and of course terrorist use of, say, engineered smallpox would blow back to kill millions of Muslims and non-Westerners.

There is debate in the expert community about whether these nightmare scenarios are plausible. But plausible or not, they are simply overshadowed for much of humanity by more immediate threats. Terrorist-engineered smallpox might kill millions, but so might natural avian flu, which stands on humanity's doorstep and is likely to race first through vulnerable societies in East and Southeast Asia. These societies lack the resources and infrastructure to contain the pandemic in its crucial early stages; if the West stepped up to fill this void, the money spent would probably save more lives than the many billions of dollars that have been devoted to the war on terror. Global climate change is another threat that could disrupt and destroy many more lives than global terrorism.[4] Of course, millions are dying already from AIDS, malaria and other infectious diseases.

Even in the early months after 11 September, when Europeans' solidarity with the United States was unreserved, it was apparent that the Bush administration's determination to put its response to the attacks within the conceptual framework of a 'war on terror' was going to be a source of transatlantic differences. The British historian Michael Howard expressed a characteristically European reaction when he wrote in *Foreign Affairs* that the US had 'made a very natural but terrible and irrevocable error' in regarding itself at war. The term 'war' conferred undue dignity and legitimacy on the terrorists, he argued, while deluding Western publics that the solution to the problem could come in the form of a military victory.[5] The main issue was political: how to deny bin Laden and his affiliates the legitimacy they were claiming, and win the hearts and minds of those whose alleged grievances they had taken up?

Any transatlantic divergence on this matter was mitigated initially by the fact that the US was engaged in a real war in Afghanistan, with participation and full support from European allies, and an Article 5 declaration of commitment from NATO. The political rift on the issue opened soon enough, however, when the term 'axis of evil' in President Bush's January 2002 State of the Union speech gave a direction and a sense of purpose to his war rhetoric which most Europeans found excessive, and worrying.[6]

The division over the language of war was an indicator of broader disagreement between the Western allies. The use of the term 'war' reflected a deep-seated strategic belief about the nature of the enemy and the struggle – often likened to the Cold War in the Bush administration's rhetoric – and the means to prevail. The doctrine of the preventive use of force as developed in the 2002 US National Security Strategy, and the Iraq War, were key elements in the American vision of the 'war on terror'.[7] This doctrine – and the choice to link it explicitly to Iraq – meant that those Europeans most opposed to the Iraq War were exposed to the spurious accusation of being soft on terrorism, with consequent damage to their political reputation among much of the American public. To their credit, governments on both sides sought to insulate their practical counter-terrorism cooperation from the fallout from the Iraq crisis. But the trans-atlantic relationship has not fully recovered from the mutual loss of confidence. For many Europeans, Iraq was at best a costly distraction from the real priorities in the fight against terrorism, at worse both a vindica-tion of the terrorist rhetoric that claims that the Muslim world is under attack from the West, and an exercise in building a training ground for future terrorist recruits. Many Americans, on the other hand, had difficulty distinguishing European opposition to the war from appeasement of the West's enemies, or visceral anti-Americanism.

Neither the war rhetoric, nor its reflection in substantive strategy, show much sign of receding from the American discourse. President Bush's introduction to the 2006 National Security Strategy starts with the words 'America is at war'.[8] The Strategy, like the 2002 edition, refers repeatedly to the ongoing 'war', and continues to discuss the war in Iraq as an aspect of the 'war' against terrorism, thus bundling together an issue which remains divisive for the transatlantic alliance with one where nothing in substance separates the allies. It insists that it is going to be a 'long war' on the model of the Cold War, and makes this the focus for the reorganisa-tion and transformation of the American military. The 'long war' concept is being elaborated throughout the US defence establishment: it is central to the Pentagon's most recent Quadrennial Defense Review, and a strategy for fighting it has been developed by US Central Command.

One cannot expect an administration whose fate has been so directly transformed by 11 September, and by the wars it launched in response, to tone down a war rhetoric so much in line with its own character[9] and, in retrospect, so important to the outcome of the 2004 election. Whether, after Bush leaves office, there will be a sea change in how the US conceptualises the struggle against terrorism is an open question. But a growing number of strategic analysts in the United States, including many with government jobs, recognise the drawbacks of a war paradigm.[10] One presidential candi-date, John Edwards, has directly challenged the value of calling it a 'war', while another, Barack Obama, has clearly subordinated the fight against terrorism under a much larger vision of national security.[11] On the other hand, there is likely to remain a political penalty for the kind of complex analysis that could be construed, however spuriously, as irresolution in the face of America's enemies. The best to be hoped for, perhaps, is a gradual de-emphasis of the war rhetoric, a conceptual disentanglement of the war in Iraq from the fight against terrorism, and a highlighting of the solid transatlantic consensus on hunting down terrorists.

The common struggle

European diffidence about a 'war on terror' corresponds neither to a lack of resolve in fighting terrorists, nor to a blanket rejection of military action as part of this fight. It reflects, rather, a conviction that situations in which military force is needed are going to be the exception rather than the rule in the course of the struggle against an enemy who wrongly claims to be at war with the West, who needs the validation of that status and whom it is therefore in the alliance's interest to characterise as a criminal foe and treat accordingly.

Europeans were not at all reluctant to fight a war in Afghanistan. It seemed to them legally and politically legitimate to chase the terrorists to their rear bases there and to destroy their Afghan state accomplices, the Taliban regime. Europe offered substantial military contributions to the Afghanistan operation, which the US for its own reasons mostly declined. European governments also subscribed to statements in NATO and the UN Security Council that effectively declared giving state support to terrorists a potential act of aggression that warranted military retaliation.

At the operational level, cooperation among Western allies against international terrorism was very strong even before the 2001 attacks. A good illustration is the case of Zacarias Moussaoui. A low-profile suspect, he was arrested by the FBI on 15 August 2001. On 21 August, responding to a request from the FBI's Minnesota field office, Paris provided intelligence it had compiled over several years, during which Moussaoui had been on a French watch list and prevented from entering France. The French informed their FBI counterparts that he had ties with radical Islamist groups and had recruited men to fight in Chechnya. They also believed that he had spent time in Afghanistan in 1999. France's timely and full sharing of intelligence does not appear to have been inhibited either by the fact that Moussaoui was a French citizen or that FBI headquarters did not seem very interested in the case.[12]

After 11 September, this already impressive level of cooperation became more intense and effective. The exchange of information improved. In France, President Chirac was reported to have instructed intelligence services to share information with American intelligence agencies 'as if they were your own service'.[13] In Germany, Chancellor Schröder declared in an official government proclamation in front of the Bundestag in October 2001 that 'President Bush reassured me how highly he and the American people value the contributions we have made so far in intelligence cooperation ... I made clear to the American president that Germany will shoulder its responsibilities in all areas. This explicitly includes military cooperation.'[14]

While real-time information exchange may be the key to effective counter-terrorist cooperation, cooperation in operations, including joint planning and execution, is also important, and it too has improved over the past six years. Indeed, while some degree of information sharing is routine, even between politically distant countries, joint operations are the truest sign of trust in intelligence cooperation. Although information in this field is scarce, collaboration appears to have reached new levels among allies after 11 September. For example, it is reported that a centre for counter-terrorist operations was established in Paris in 2002 by the US, France, Britain, Germany, Canada and Australia. The role of the centre, believed to be called 'Alliance Base', is to analyse the transnational movement of terrorist suspects and develop operations to spy on and catch them.[15]

Continental European allies have also been involved in counter-terrorist operations involving military forces: naval control operations in the Indian Ocean following the demise of the Taliban in Afghanistan are a case in point, likewise the commitment of European special forces to counter-terrorist operations under US command in the war in Afghanistan – during the first phase in 2002 alongside the Northern Alliance, and from 2003 onwards in the south of the country, where German, and later French special forces are reported to have operated alongside the Americans.[16]

Little of this quiet cooperation has been publicised, or politically recognised. It should be noted, however, that even in the early months of 2003 – the most acute period of alliance acrimony over Iraq – political leaders confirmed that counter-terrorist cooperation would continue unchanged.[17] (The single, notable exception was then-US Defense Secretary Donald Rumsfeld, who decided to restrict military-to-military contact and access to intelligence originating from the Pentagon, as part of a strategy of retaliation against those allies who most strongly opposed the war in Iraq. These restrictions, had they been extended to other government departments, and fully, rather than reluctantly, implemented by those in charge, could well have impaired allied counter-terrorist operations.)

Yet, although counter-terrorism cooperation is strong, there are difficulties. International cooperation against terrorism develops at three main levels: intelligence-sharing, police and judicial cooperation, and military action. The first is, necessarily, an opaque process that does not lend itself to a public display of harmony among allies, however good the cooperation may be in substance. The second is intrinsically cumbersome and vulnerable to divisions: police and judicial cooperation is constrained by diverse legal and constitutional rules, and depends on the assent of national judiciaries, which do not yield easily to the demands of international counter-terrorism cooperation. This is very difficult territory, among Europeans as well as across the Atlantic.

The inevitable invisibility of most strands of counter-terrorist cooperation can encourage misperceptions on both sides, in particular American prejudices that Europeans are insufficiently mobilised against terrorism. Furthermore, conceptual differences may compromise interests which remain convergent at the more practical level. Even where there is common action, such as in the day-to-day fight against global jihadist networks, transatlantic differences of perspective can jeopardise cooperation. In democracies, it is difficult to continue with practical police, judicial and intelligence cooperation against terrorism while having differences on law enforcement policies that resonate deeply in public opinions (Guantanamo, renditions, the interpretation of the Geneva Conventions, the prohibition of torture).

'Root causes'

The question of 'root causes' poses difficult dilemmas for both the United States and Europe. There is an understandable inclination to ignore the underlying political and social grievances which fuel terrorism, to depict the enemy as an embodiment of 'evil' whose motives need not be understood, because understanding would be the first step towards justifying its actions. But there are risks in depicting terrorism as an abstract and uniquely malevolent disease to be fought, rather than the reflection of real problems to be addressed.

International relations scholar Adam Roberts has reminded us that in the 1950s and 1960s a similarly narrow characterisation was developed by analysts in charge of counter-insurgency operations in Malaya and Indochina. The concept of 'revolutionary war' blinded them to important dimensions of the fight (nationalism in particular), with serious consequences for the counter-insurgency effort. In addition, by designating the threat in abstract terms, unrelated to political and human realities, it conceptually paved the way for the use of unacceptable tactics and methods, including torture.

There is, however, no denying the danger of entering a vicious cycle wherein political concessions vindicate the choice of violent tactics in the eyes of extremists, thus emboldening rather than weakening terrorism. In some cases, this risk has been minimised by limiting the political process to the part of the movement least committed to violence (the so-called 'political branch') in tandem with the repression of its most desperate elements. This is more or less the strategy that brought about the Good Friday Agreement in Northern Ireland. Roberts stresses that several terrorist campaigns of the past were ended only by a combination of successful repression and political attention to the underlying grievances.[18]

None of these issues are easy, morally or politically. Nevertheless, there are some basic principles that can guide policymakers. Firstly, action to address 'root causes' is not aimed at changing the minds of the terrorists, but at winning the hearts and minds of the community whose interests the terrorist movement purports to serve. Secondly, when confronted with serious grievances and political problems, refusing to address them for fear of 'rewarding terrorism' can be self-defeating. It must always be better to fix problems than to leave them to fester. That fact that one of bin Laden's foremost complaints was the American presence in Saudi Arabia has not deterred the United States from removing its troops, for its own good reasons.

Thirdly, addressing root causes is not a substitute for chasing terrorists. Both courses of action should be conducted in parallel, with the overarching objective of delegitimising terrorism. Capture and defeat takes away some of the prestige of terrorists by demonstrating that their activity is ineffective and even dangerous for the cause or the community they claim to serve. Terrorism can be further discredited if the problems it aims to highlight are effectively dealt with by credible political processes.

Finally, there are different levels of underlying cause: from clear-cut political grievances that can be addressed, to social and ideological currents that are not amenable to plausible treatment in any depth. Aspirations to greater political autonomy, or statehood, on the part of national independence movements fall in the former category. The visions that animated the Red Brigades or the Red Army Faction in the 1970s, for example, fall into the latter. While every kind of terrorism has underlying causes, some lend themselves to a political response of a kind, others do not. Millenarian groups, apocalyptic cults and other perpetrators of senseless violence cannot be appeased politically. No one would blame the Japanese or US governments for failing to address the root causes of the terrorist violence perpetrated by the Aum Shinrikyo cult or the Oklahoma City bomber Timothy McVeigh.

Global Islamist terrorism presents unique challenges in this regard. It borrows features from disparate types of terrorist movement: the intractable and irrational qualities (including the resort to suicide) and religious inspiration of violent cults, and the nationalist agenda of national liberation movements (in this case, freeing the Middle East from the presence and domination of the West); and combines them with a belief in the existence of a civil war, initially within the Arab world between 'apostate' pro-Western regimes and the true believers, eventually extending to Southeast Asia, Europe and everywhere Muslims are 'oppressed'.

Faced with this uniquely challenging mixture, neither the Europeans nor the Americans have deluded themselves that al-Qaeda operatives, their active supporters or immediate followers could be lured out of their terrorist activities by any direct political engagement. Yet whether their movement is an extreme and marginal phenomenon on the fringes of the Muslim world, or is widely regarded as speaking to its grievances and deserving its admiration and support, will make an enormous difference to the outcome of this fight. Of course, any strategy for countering the influence of terrorists in the Muslim world will largely be determined by how one chooses to characterise its problems. These are difficult issues, on which there is no unified opinion on either side of the Atlantic.

There are, however, different tendencies at work. It is fair to say that, as a general proposition, European analysts and publics have been more favourably disposed towards the notion of 'root causes' and have more easily recognised the need to address them as part of the fight against terrorism. In the immediate aftermath of 11 September, the American public was reluctant to acknowledge that there might be 'reasons' behind what was so clearly an unjustifiable and monstrous act of blind hatred. Rather than to 'causes', therefore, the US government referred to 'underlying conditions' that made terrorism more likely, and hence needed to be addressed. By contrast, the UK Government in its 2002 *Strategic Defence Review: A New Chapter* was more blunt in stating: 'countering terrorism is usually a long-term business requiring the roots and causes to be addressed as well as the symptoms'.[19]

Subsequently, the United States has gone some way to broaden its strategy against terrorism, and identify its fundamental causes. However, even this expanded approach has serious limitations. To understand the problem, it is worth quoting at some length from the Bush administration's 2006 National Security Strategy:

> To wage this battle of ideas effectively, we must be clear-eyed about what does and does not give rise to terrorism:
> - Terrorism is not the inevitable by-product of poverty. Many of the September 11 hijackers were from middle-class backgrounds, and many terrorist leaders, like bin Laden, are from privileged upbringings.
> - Terrorism is not simply a result of hostility to U.S. policy in Iraq. The United States was attacked on September 11 and earlier, well before we toppled the Saddam Hussein regime. Moreover, countries that stayed out of the Iraq war have not been spared from terror attack.
> - Terrorism is not simply a result of Israeli–Palestinian issues. Al-Qaida plotting for the September 11 attacks began in the 1990s, during an active period in the peace process.
> - Terrorism is not simply a response to our efforts to prevent terror attacks. The al-Qaida network targeted the United States long before the United States targeted al-Qaida. Indeed, the terrorists are emboldened more by perceptions of weakness than by demonstrations of resolve. Terrorists lure recruits by telling them that we are decadent and easily intimidated and will retreat if attacked.
>
> The terrorism we confront today springs from:
> - Political alienation. Transnational terrorists are recruited from people who have no voice in their own government and see no legitimate way to promote change in their own country. Without a stake in the existing order, they are vulnerable to manipulation by those who advocate a perverse vision based on violence and destruction.
> - Grievances that can be blamed on others. The failures the terrorists feel and see are blamed on others, and on perceived injustices from the recent or sometimes distant past. The terrorists' rhetoric keeps wounds associated with this past fresh and raw, a potent motivation for revenge and terror.
> - Sub-cultures of conspiracy and misinformation. Terrorists recruit more effectively from populations whose information about the world is contaminated by falsehoods and corrupted by conspiracy theories. The distortions keep alive grievances and filter out facts that would challenge popular prejudices and self-serving propaganda.

- An ideology that justifies murder. Terrorism ultimately depends upon the appeal of an ideology that excuses or even glorifies the deliberate killing of innocents. A proud religion – the religion of Islam – has been twisted and made to serve an evil end, as in other times and places other religions have been similarly abused.

Defeating terrorism in the long run requires that each of these factors be addressed. The genius of democracy is that it provides a counter to each.

- In place of alienation, democracy offers an ownership stake in society, a chance to shape one's own future.
- In place of festering grievances, democracy offers the rule of law, the peaceful resolution of disputes, and the habits of advancing interests through compromise.
- In place of a culture of conspiracy and misinformation, democracy offers freedom of speech, independent media, and the marketplace of ideas, which can expose and discredit falsehoods, prejudices, and dishonest propaganda.
- In place of an ideology that justifies murder, democracy offers a respect for human dignity that abhors the deliberate targeting of innocent civilians.

Democracy is the opposite of terrorist tyranny, which is why the terrorists denounce it and are willing to kill the innocent to stop it. Democracy is based on empowerment, while the terrorists' ideology is based on enslavement. Democracies expand the freedom of their citizens, while the terrorists seek to impose a single set of narrow beliefs. Democracy sees individuals as equal in worth and dignity, having an inherent potential to create and to govern themselves. The terrorists see individuals as objects to be exploited, and then to be ruled and oppressed.

Democracies are not immune to terrorism. In some democracies, some ethnic or religious groups are unable or unwilling to grasp the benefits of freedom otherwise available in the society. Such groups can evidence the same alienation and despair that the transnational terrorists exploit in undemocratic states. This accounts for the emergence in democratic societies of home-grown terrorists such as were responsible for the bombings in London in July 2005 and for the violence in some other nations. Even in these cases, the long-term solution remains deepening the reach of democracy so that all citizens enjoy its benefits.[20]

This analysis essentially identifies one main underlying cause of terrorism, 'political alienation', and only one remedy, democracy. The text begins by dismissing four commonly suggested root causes of contemporary terrorism and goes on to propose what it regards as the four true causes, three of which it then effectively discards as devious, with such words as 'rhetoric', 'falsehood' and 'ideology', leaving only 'political alienation' standing as a genuine cause.

The methodological problem with such an approach is that it is primarily concerned with the motives of the terrorists themselves, which may indeed be disingenuous. But the fight against terrorism is not just a bilateral contest. Rather, it is a trilateral struggle with a critical third party in the middle – the body politic in whose name the terrorists claim to act. While addressing 'root causes' is probably going to make little difference with respect to the terrorists themselves, it may exert a potent influence on the attitude of Arabs and Muslims across the world.

While it is probably correct that political alienation is the main root cause of terrorism, this diagnosis gives little guide as to the course of action best suited to influencing the attitude of this third party. It remains at a level of generality which allows it to overlook the actual existence of perceptions and grievances, related to real events, among many people in the Middle East and beyond, that feed Islamist extremism and global jihadist terrorism: the sense that the region has been abused in the past by great power politics, and continues to be subject to excessive American influence and interference; the resulting feeling of abuse and wounded pride; the acute sense of injustice which stems from the perception that this American interference, justified under the guise of universal legal rules and moral principles, is in fact biased in favour of Israel; the corresponding perception that Israel is not held by the West to the same standards as the rest of the region on subjects including proliferation, the admissibility of the acquisition of territory by force and the treatment of civilians under occupation; and finally, the merging of these various grievances, which have a nationalistic character, with a powerful sense of religious identity, and of religious polarisation with the West, despite Western pronouncements to the contrary.

European alertness to the role played by these kinds of 'root causes' is certainly sensible; equally, however, Americans may be more realistic about the limited feasibility of addressing such causes within a time frame relevant to the immediate threat. Americans and Europeans should nevertheless be able to agree on the importance of avoiding actions that make the problem worse by sharpening the polarisation between the West and the Muslim world, and bringing about precisely what bin Laden and his affiliates are seeking: a 'war' between a significant portion of the Muslim world and the West.

The limits of democracy

Against this background, one can better understand European apprehensions about promoting democracy as the centrepiece of the 'root causes' element of the West's counter-terrorist strategies. No European leader would deny that promoting human rights, the rule of law and democracy in the Middle East is desirable. But there are limits to and potentially undesirable effects of using democracy promotion as a strategy for fighting terrorism.

The first is related to the role that nationalism might play in any polarisation of Islam and the West. Democracy and nationalism go together. Especially in early phases of transition to democracy, nationalism is a potent political resource, which is easily mobilised in its extreme forms, as was evidenced in the early 1990s in the former Yugoslavia and in sub-Saharan Africa, and is now in Iraq. Anti-Western and especially anti-American nationalism is so prevalent today in the Middle East as to warrant caution on this front.

Genuine democracy is no guarantee against Islamist extremism, and may even make the problem worse. After Israel, the freest electoral processes in the Middle East are to be found in Iraq, the Palestinian territories and, to a lesser extent, Iran. The November 2005 Egyptian elections were marked by an improved degree of transparency and fairness. In all four places, recent elections have witnessed the rise of Islamist extremist forces, and anti-Western and anti-American attitudes have been shown to be as potent as ever. These are four very different and specific cases, to be sure, but they highlight the difficulties and contradictions of the Western approach to democracy in the Middle East. These contradictions are most conspicuous in relation to the Palestinian Authority (PA). Following Hamas's election victory in January 2006 and the ensuing suspension of Western aid to the PA, it is only too easy for the adversaries of the West to insist that it favours democracy in the Middle East only when it likes the outcome, and punishes those who do not vote according to its wishes.

The second reason for caution is the limited influence outsiders have over internal political processes, and over authoritarian regimes. For all their shortcomings, and brutality, Middle Eastern regimes have proven exceptionally durable and resilient. They have shown considerable deftness in deflecting external pressures aimed at bringing about more

openness and political fairness, including by mobilising nationalist senti-
ments against those who try to modify their conduct. External support
may be the kiss of death for democratic movements, whose embrace by the
West may make them easier targets for authoritarian regimes and extremist movements.

There is a certain surreal quality to the discussion in the West of democracy in the Middle East, in view of the little impact, one way or the other,
of Western policies in this respect. There were passionate debates in France
and elsewhere on how to react to the suspension of the electoral process
by the military following the victory of the Islamic Salvation Front in the
first turn of the 1991 elections in Algeria, and, later, on whether and how
to bring about an end to the ensuing civil war through dialogue between
the parties. These debates contrasted with the local parties' determination,
embarked as they were on a life-or-death struggle, to conduct the fight on
their own terms, and not to yield to outside interference of any kind. The
mere suspicion of outsiders' willingness to bring their influence to bear on
the course of events brought about the most violent reactions against them
from both sides. In the end, no one but the Algerians contenders themselves decided the outcome of the struggle.

Democracy promotion is always desirable as a matter of principle. It
should be pursued in the Middle East as elsewhere, to the degree to which
Western influence and security interests allow. As a tool for crafting a solution to the problem of jihadist terrorism, however, it is likely to be of little
immediate use, and might have unintended and unwelcome effects.

Terror, rights and the rule of law

While the desirability of the revolutionary promotion of democracy
in pursuit of a radically reordered state and society might be in doubt,
the importance of defending basic human rights, which it is possible to
attempt even within authoritarian societies, is clear. When it comes to
human rights, it is a truism that the West's own probity and reputation for
upholding its best values is the *sine qua non* for any effort to export those
values elsewhere. In this regard, the American failure and abdication of
the past several years – with the complicity of some European governments – is stark.

No issue has more potential to damage alliance purposes and under-
mine cooperation against terrorism than the treatment of prisoners. To
be fair, there is now a passionate debate on these issues in the United
States, where the most outrageous propositions relating to the treatment
of prisoners in the 'war on terror' – for the legal admissibility of humili-

ating and degrading treatment, if not outright torture, and detention at will without judicial review – have been challenged, with a measure of success, by a coalition which includes a more resolute Democratic Party; influential voices within the Republican Party, such as that of Senator John McCain; an increasingly assertive court system; and a growing portion of the American public that worries about the country's moral reputation.

European governments have done little to confront Washington on these issues. The British government seems to have been the most active and vocal in seeking to resolve the cases of those of its citizens detained at Guantanamo Bay. The French government has been slow to react to the situation of French detainees, and incarcerated and indicted some of them in France upon their release by the Americans for belonging to a 'terrorist conspiracy', even though they appear not to have participated in serious terrorist activities.[21]

We have witnessed, in fact, an unhappy convergence of transatlantic policy: an explicit US and tacit European lowering of human rights and due process standards in the fight against terrorism. Council of Europe inquiries into the issue of illegal abductions and transfers of terrorist suspects in Europe as part of the American practice of 'renditions' seem to indicate that a number of European governments, or at least agencies within them, have been quietly acquiescent in or actively supportive of the practice.[22] The hypocrisy of a number of European governments in effectively accepting the predicament of their nationals in Guantanamo and illegal abductions of alleged terrorists on their soil is not the contribution to transatlantic relations that we need. It shows that in the long run the 'war on terror' can harm the transatlantic alliance, not only where allies differ, but just as much where they agree on policies that are alien to the democratic values that ought to cement their alliance together.

Meanwhile, the judgement of European publics of American practices and doctrines related to the treatment of terrorist suspects, in Iraq and elsewhere, has been damning. This is largely an American-made problem, from which the Americans will have to extricate themselves, and there is little their allies can do to help. Perhaps the perceived estrangement of the US from other Western opinions on this issue will be of some use in this, in reinforcing the arguments of those Americans who stand for a reversal of the most excessive practices of the US administration.

The social geography of terrorism
United in fighting terrorism, Europe and the US nevertheless see it from different geographical and societal perspectives. Equally, Americans and

Europeans are not seen in exactly the same way by the terrorist movements which they confront.

There is a common view, laid out at the beginning of this chapter, that conveys these real differences. The US, it has been said, is confronted with an external threat, from which the Americans have sought to insulate themselves with physical protection at home and aggressive action abroad. The Europeans, by contrast, are confronted with an internal threat emerging from the midst of their large Muslim communities. They cannot insulate themselves from this threat, which US success in 'hardening' its territory makes even more pressing.

The reality is, of course, somewhat more complicated, as informal discussions with counter-terrorist officials in Europe make clear that most are acutely aware of the external threat to Europe, from al-Qaeda, affiliated groups in the Middle East, and other groups, such as Hizbullah, should they choose to go on the offensive. The bombings in London and Madrid seem to have been conducted by largely indigenous groups, but the inspiration and ideological motives came from the wider al-Qaeda network. Major attacks thwarted in France – against Strasbourg Cathedral and the US embassy in Paris – were planned by external groups. Equally, the home-grown terrorist threat inside the US may have been underestimated.

It is nonetheless a real possibility that the combination of the bolstering of US homeland security and the contiguity of Europe to the Muslim world – both geographically and through the presence of large immigrant communities from South Asia, the Middle East and North Africa – will turn Europe into the main area of attraction for global jihadist activities. This possibility harbours a rich potential for transatlantic confusion and tensions. The suspicion that the Europeans' attitude towards the Middle East might be influenced unduly by their Muslim minorities can already be heard in some segments of American opinion. Americans often flatly associate the discontent of immigrant communities in Europe with Islamist militancy. The urban riots that took place in the autumn of 2005 in France were presented in numerous American media as another 'intifada', although in fact they were essentially void of any religious, ideological or foreign policy motive.[23]

Models for integrating immigrants within society vary greatly from country to country and are intrinsic to national identities. The terrorist threat emanating from a given country's Muslim minority may be blamed on perceived weaknesses in that country's treatment of immigrants, or on its poor integration model. Some American analysts ascribe the lack of internal terrorist threat in the United States to the better integration of Muslims into American society.[24]

In the world of global terrorism, no threat is purely local. In a certain sense this makes every country accountable for letting a terrorist threat develop on its territory, and invites judgements on the part of others about policies that could create the conditions for its development. Europeans may be right to point to the enabling effect that the Bush administration's Middle East policies have had on jihadist terrorism. They are not shy to point to their own deeper understanding of the Muslim world, which is more questionable. On these issues, some degree of mutual recrimination is unavoidable. Allies should take care, however, not to let it weaken the sense of solidarity in the face of a shared threat.

CHAPTER TWO

Confronting Proliferation

The transatlantic train wreck of 2003 was an argument between Americans and most Europeans about the wisdom and legitimacy of a second war against Iraq. It seemed for many to portend a fundamental, perhaps irrevocable, rupture of transatlantic relations. Then, however, the *casus belli* – Baghdad's proscribed weapons programmes – evaporated. The occupation by coalition forces turned quickly into a counter-insurgency quagmire, and more gradually into a holding action against civil war. As a consequence, most Americans have come to agree with most Europeans about the wisdom, if not the legitimacy, of the original adventure. This reconvergence of views undermines the notion that there is something structural and inevitable about the transatlantic crisis. As Francis Fukuyama has argued:

> neither American political culture nor any underlying domestic pressures or constraints have determined the key decisions in American foreign policy since Sept. 11. In the immediate aftermath of the 9/11 attacks, Americans would have allowed President Bush to lead them in any of several directions, and the nation was prepared to accept substantial risks and sacrifices. The Bush administration asked for no sacrifices from the average American, but after the quick fall of the Taliban it rolled the dice in a big way by moving to solve a longstanding problem only tangentially related to the threat from Al Qaeda – Iraq.[1]

It remains true, however, that the Iraq disagreement was compounded by enduring differences in the prevailing European and American approaches to proliferation threats. These differences became apparent soon after the end of the Cold War. An influential current in American strategic thought came early to the conclusion, as expressed by neo-conservative writer Charles Krauthammer, that the most potent post-Cold War threats would be in the form of 'weapons states' – rogue dictatorships, such as Iraq or North Korea, whose prestige and potency derived from their pursuit of unconventional, especially nuclear, weapons programmes.[2] It was said to be in the nature of such regimes that they were opaque risk-takers: prone to miscalculation because they were sealed off from international society's normal, rational discourse; inhumane towards their own people as well as adversaries; and therefore, in too many plausible scenarios, not amenable to the Cold War principles of nuclear deterrence.

In reality, the extent of nuclear proliferation was remarkably contained, compared to John F. Kennedy's 1963 warning of 15 to 25 nuclear powers within a decade. Three decades after his prediction, there were only five declared nuclear weapons states (the US, UK, France, Russia and China), along with three states (Israel, Pakistan and India) widely thought to be pursuing covert nuclear-weapons programmes. By the 1990s, however, there was some reason to worry that the dam might burst. Iraq's nuclear programme had made alarming progress before being interrupted by the 1991 war. North Korea, after its plutonium-based programme was discovered in 1993, was locked for the rest of the decade into an unsettling game of confrontation and sullen negotiation with the US. In 1998, India and Pakistan both tested nuclear devices and came close, arguably, to nuclear war. It was later learned that A.Q. Khan, father of Pakistan's enrichment programme, had set up a clandestine international market in nuclear weapons know-how that included North Korea, Libya and Iran, and possibly other countries as well.[3]

The Clinton administration did not share much of the Krauthammer worldview, but it did consider Baghdad's apparent ongoing efforts at surreptitious rearmament to pose a threat to American and international security that required a military response. As Saddam Hussein's scientific establishment played cat-and-mouse with UN arms inspectors throughout the 1990s, and as the UN sanctions regime appeared to fray, the Security Council fractured along the lines that were to be repeated in the full rupture of spring 2003. In 1998, the US and Britain conducted an intensive bombing campaign against sites in Iraq related to suspected WMD programmes, in response to Iraqi restrictions on international inspections. The fierce debate between the US and the UK on one hand and France and Russia on the other over this campaign rehearsed many of the arguments that were to be repeated five years later. In 1998 as in 2003, the Americans and British insisted that they were enforcing UN resolutions calling on Iraq to disarm completely and to cooperate fully with the inspections regime. According to Washington and London, the credibility of the Security Council was at stake; if the Security Council as a whole was not willing to enforce its own Chapter Seven resolutions,[4] then individual members had to do so. This line of argument was bound to run into resistance, along the lines expressed by Cambridge University legal scholar Marc Weller:

> It is obvious that a general right of states to appoint themselves the executors of the 'will' of the Security Council would lead to very significant instability. To appreciate this point, one only needs to flick through the 1,000-plus Security Council resolutions and identify the numerous situations where the 'will' of the Council has not been fully and unconditionally complied with. Even in relation to the significantly smaller number of demands of the Council made in the context of Chapter VII, this theory would be immediately rejected by the US and UK if it were advanced by other states. In fact, it would be very difficult for the Security Council to adopt any sort of resolution at all, if the very fact of the expression of the 'will' of the Council were taken to imply a mandate to enforce it militarily.[5]

Yet, though Weller's complaint was powerful, it hardly answered the worry about what to do if the UN Security Council could not agree to confront dire threats to international peace and security. The failure to reach a Security Council or transatlantic consensus on this matter was perhaps tolerable so long as one or both of the following conditions prevailed: countries such as France and Russia were willing to swallow the occasional unilateral military action by the United States and a coalition of the willing, or, conversely, the United States concluded that the WMD activities of 'rogue states' such as Iraq and North Korea were unnerving but manageable.

This rough agreement to disagree could not, however, easily survive the nightmare vision of catastrophic insecurity that confronted America after the terrorist destruction of the World Trade Center. The smouldering hole in lower Manhattan prompted an obvious question: what if these terrorists could acquire a nuclear weapon?

It is clear enough from the perspective of 2007 – and indeed, there were plenty of warnings at the time – that invading Iraq was not a sensible answer to this question. But the question remains, and has the potential to continue to divide America from Europe.

It will be divisive, in the first instance, if Iran appears to be on the verge of acquiring a nuclear-weapons capability or building a nuclear weapon. Many analysts on both sides of the Atlantic are sceptical that the Iranian regime, despite its history of working with terrorists, would hand over nuclear technology to actors that are beyond its full control, or that the regime itself would launch a suicidal nuclear attack against Israel or the United States. Yet this scepticism is not sufficiently reassuring to the Israeli public or American politicians. Politically, then, if not analytically, America and Europe have very different threat perceptions. The '1% doctrine' – the idea, attributed to Vice President Dick Cheney, that if there is a 1% chance of terrorists acquiring nuclear weapons, the US must treat it as a certainty – will continue to influence the US debate on proliferation and terrorism, even if American policies currently seem more subdued because of the problems in Iraq.[6] The fact that A.Q. Khan, a prominent scientist working for a state more or less aligned with the United States, would sell nuclear technology to regimes as erratic as North Korea's, reinforces the argument that states cannot be expected always to act in rational ways. Iran's government is not necessarily any more of a single rational actor than Pakistan – it too has competing centres of authority, a 'Supreme Leader' and an elected president, intelligence services and Revolutionary Guards with, arguably, their own agendas and their own relationships with terrorist groups such as Hizbullah.

Yet the problem with any kind of 1% doctrine – that is, with any policy approach based on the assumption that where the consequences could be catastrophic, the relative likelihood is irrelevant – has been demonstrated in Iraq. A war fought against the mere possibility of a collaborative relationship between a hostile regime and jihadist terrorists, and to forestall a future potential of nuclear and biological armament, has palpably worsened the risks to the United States and its allies. The presence of al-Qaeda-linked terrorists in Iraq, fictional before the war, is now a reality, and the leverage against Iranian nuclear ambitions has diminished dramatically.

There is no plausible transatlantic consensus on non-proliferation or counter-proliferation that will fully answer America's worst fears about nuclear or biological attack by state or terrorist enemies. But nor is there a unilateral strategy that can fully answer those fears. What should be sought, then, is an overlapping, if not always concerted, transatlantic agenda for long-term action to counter as many of the most likely risks as possible.

Pre-emption and preventive war

As transatlantic partners seek such an agenda, one thing is clear: no transatlantic consensus can be formed around preventive war as a doctrine.

There has been a pernicious confusion of terms between 'prevention' – the use of force against a potential threat that is not yet imminent – and 'pre-emption' against an imminent threat. In the debate of recent years these terms have often been used interchangeably, adding to the confusion.

Between 11 September 2001 and the 20 March 2003 invasion of Iraq, the White House staked out in a series of speeches and strategy documents its claim that the United States could use force against certain countries before those countries presented an actual threat. Whatever the strategic merits of such a proposition, they are bound to be lost on a community of countries in whose collective interest it is to uphold the normative prohibition of the use of force as laid out in the UN Charter.

That an international consensus cannot be built around the principle of preventive war does not mean that states cannot, or even should not, strike first. There is, to begin with, a well recognised right in international law to 'pre-emptive self-defence' – that is, a right to strike first to forestall an imminent attack. 'If an army is mobilising, its capacity to cause damage clear and its hostile intentions unequivocal, nobody has ever seriously suggested that you have to wait to be fired upon', as former Australian Foreign Minister Gareth Evans, a leading member of the UN secretary-general's 'High Level Panel on Threats, Challenges and Change', has observed.[7] It is, moreover, reasonable to argue that the advent of nuclear and biological weapons, and the stated intentions of terrorist groups to acquire them, blurs the distinction between pre-emptive war against an imminent threat and preventive war against a future, potential threat. It is not unsustainable to suggest that military action might have to be taken against states seeking to acquire weapons of mass destruction before an actual threat materialises, either in order to prevent them from turning these weapons over to terrorists, or simply because the mere possession of such weapons by unreliable or aggressive states is a grave concern for world peace. It was in 1992 that a Security Council summit meeting first designated weapons proliferation a threat to peace and international security, and signalled its resolve to meet that threat with coercive action if necessary, much as force had been used against Iraq in the first Gulf War the year before.

Nothing in the UN Charter restricts the Security Council from undertaking or authorising preventive action, including preventive military action, as part of its mandate to maintain international peace and security. The Security Council has, in fact, gone a long way, especially since 11 September, to uphold such action when it has been directly and clearly related to either proliferation or international terrorism. It sanctioned the US and allied actions in Afghanistan. (This was, to be sure, a war of retaliation, but it was also preventive self-defence against future terrorism.) It established through a series of resolutions mandatory international legislation forbidding state assistance of, and acquiescence in, terrorist activities, and has thus established a presumption that states failing to comply with these obligations would expose themselves to sanctions, including military force.

The use of force against proliferating states remains an option, and no one has ever been in any doubt that the US government in particular would keep this option open, especially against the background of a possible convergence of global terrorist movements with nuclear or biological weapons. European governments understand that the US needs to retain this option, and some have even hinted that they might themselves consider pre-emptive measures, including nuclear options, should extreme circumstances of terrorist threats associated with such weapons arise.[8]

Preventive war as an overarching doctrine, however, as it is laid out in the 2002 US National Security Strategy, and restated in 2006, poses at least two problems. Firstly, it would tend to establish making war as a normative option for dealing with proliferators. This directly challenges the norm of non-use of force. Most countries would resign themselves to seeing this norm put aside under exceptional circumstances. In retrospect, for example, many now accept that the bombing in 1981 of Iraq's Osirak nuclear reactor was not, on balance, a bad thing (though it is questionable whether it in fact slowed down Iraq's quest for nuclear weapons).[9] But the same countries are unwilling to see the establishment of a doctrine that would give enormous leeway to the United States to disregard the prohibition on the use of force as it saw fit. If the United States were granted this freedom, it could not easily be denied to other major powers, leading to a world in which the strong waged war on the weak.

The second and related problem is that Iraq has shown that the Americans can be grossly mistaken in their assessments of the emerging WMD/terrorist threats that the preventive use of force doctrine is intended to cover. If there was any chance of progress toward an international acceptance of the doctrine, it was lost in Iraq, along with a good deal of confidence in the United States' ultimate motives for enunciating it in the first place. Similarly, domestic American support for the doctrine has been a casualty of Iraq.

Preventive war is both too dogmatic and too deeply intertwined with the argument over the Iraq War to be rescued as a basis for a future transatlantic or international consensus. It still should be possible, however, to make better political use of the body of counter-terrorist international legislation that was passed by the Security Council in the aftermath of 11 September to isolate, intimidate and if necessary coerce those states tempted to support global terrorism. The degree of consensus already achieved has been unfortunately obfuscated by the debate on the preventive or pre-emptive resort to force. Putting that debate aside should help rejuvenate this consensus, in both transatlantic and broader international terms.

Iran

This consensus is critical to dealing with Iranian nuclear ambitions. Iran is by far the most important nuclear proliferation issue facing Europe and America, and it sets critical tests for the allies. One is of the ability of the collective security system to fulfil its function in practice. Having in 1992 formally acknowledged the threat posed to international peace and security by WMD proliferation, can the Security Council now deal effectively with the real-world threat from Iran? Will it be possible to successfully use diplomacy and pressure to dissuade a resourceful, determined country from acquiring nuclear weapons, before recourse to force becomes necessary? The crisis is also the most important test case for transatlantic cooperation post-Iraq.

In contrast to the divisions over Iraq, the transatlantic allies agree on the essential nature of the threat and the most desirable strategy for seeking a solution. They share a common assessment that Iran is seeking a nuclear-weapons capability, but is still probably some time away from achieving that objective. The intelligence agencies of the major transatlantic powers have developed the habit of sharing information and analysis, which has helped to promote the coordination of diplomatic strategies.

The allies also agree that if Iran achieved its nuclear objectives, it would pose a devastating threat to the NPT regime and Middle Eastern stability. In general, the Europeans tend to place most emphasis on the threat to the international non-proliferation regime. Iran, despite being found in non-compliance with its IAEA safeguards agreement, is seeking to defy the will of the UN Security Council and develop a nuclear-weapons capability under the guise of its 'rights' to a peaceful nuclear programme. If it succeeds in this, it will expose, if not a fundamental weakness in the NPT, then at least a fundamental lack of political will in upholding this vital norm – thus inviting other countries to follow Iran's precedent. While sharing this concern, many Americans focus on the additional danger that a nuclear-armed Iran might pose an existential threat to Israel or transfer nuclear weapons or materials to terrorist groups. In any event, Americans and Europeans agree that Iran's acquisition of a nuclear-weapons capability would spur further proliferation in the region and that a nuclear-armed Iran is likely to be even more aggressive in pursuing regional dominance, which would threaten Western energy and geopolitical interests in the region.

Against this threat, the allies have come to agreement on a basic diplomatic strategy, in the form of a two-track approach – a substantial package of incentives for Iran to agree to long-term suspension of enrichment-related and reprocessing activities, backed by the threat of increasing economic and political sanctions if it continues in these activities. Moreover, the allies have worked together to convince Russia and China to adopt this strategy, managing to transform transatlantic cooperation into a Security Council Permanent 5 (P5) + Germany (or, more precisely, historically speaking, an E3+3) approach, backed by the legal authority of the Security Council. The past five years have been quite successful: determined European action has attracted the United States on the one hand, China and Russia on the other, toward this two-track approach of muscular multilateral diplomacy.

As long as this strategy appears to have reasonable prospects for success – and Iran remains below the critical threshold of a nuclear-weapons capability – transatlantic cooperation will remain strong – especially if a defiant President Ahmadinejad-led government remains in power. If, however, Iran continues to defy Security Council demands that it suspend its enrichment programme (a condition for holding negotiations with the P5 + Germany), and if it overcomes the technical problems that plague the programme, a new rift may open in the alliance. The allies could once again come to a parting of the ways, particularly if, in addition, a more sensible Iranian government comes to power, blurring lines that have been clearly drawn, and, for the moment, held. Washington is prepared, in extremis, to undertake military attacks on Iran's nuclear facilities, while the European capitals are more sensitive to the cost of a military option.

Negotiating history

Iran's secret nuclear fuel-cycle programme became public in August 2002, at the same time as the allies were beginning to argue about the upcoming

Iraq War. After the war had begun, in the summer and autumn of 2003, a French, German and UK initiative (E3) was launched in relation to Iran, which linked together various disparate concerns and goals: a genuine belief that an Iranian nuclear capability posed significant threats to the Middle East, Europe and the global order; a determination to show that the EU was 'serious' and, importantly after the Iraq crisis, united in confronting such challenges; and (not incidentally) a wish to avoid being led into another Iraq-style crisis on strictly American terms.[10] Ironically, the very success of the Coalition invasion of Iraq created favourable conditions for E3 diplomatic efforts. Fearing that it was next on Washington's 'axis of evil' hit list, Tehran saw its negotiations with Europe as a means to avoid referral to the Security Council and reduce the risks of economic sanctions, political isolation and military attack.

It would seem that some Iranians also thought it might be possible to divide the E3 along familiar lines, and divide them from the Americans, by cutting a deal with the Europeans that allowed Iran to retain its enrichment programme – subject to some technical and political limitations – thus undermining US demands for 'permanent suspension'. Because Tehran misread the motivations for European involvement, it mistakenly believed that it would be able to play up the divisions that appeared during the Iraq crisis, drive a wedge between Europeans, between Europeans and Americans, and between the West on the one hand and Russia and China on the other.

But the E3's determination and ability to stay the course they had set out for themselves in 2003 proved key in consolidating the unity of the international community in the years that followed, bringing together Washington, Moscow and Beijing, first in support of, and then as part of, the EU strategy. This unity of the P5 was in turn instrumental in drawing in key non-aligned countries, which has allowed for two unanimously adopted sanctions resolutions.

At first, the United States had been suspicious of, if not outright hostile towards, the E3 negotiations. In 2003, it repeatedly argued, through the voice of Under Secretary for Arms Control and International Security Affairs John Bolton, in favour of an immediate referral to the Security Council. It was hard, however, for Washington to gainsay the Europeans' apparent successes, other than to predict that the 2003 and 2004 suspension agreements would not hold. Despite Washington's misgivings, the US could not win a vote of the 35-member IAEA Board of Governors to refer Iran to the Security Council without the Europeans, and the E3 skilfully used the threat of referral to force Iran to accept a suspension of further key elements of its enrichment activities and to cooperate with the IAEA in revealing details of its clandestine nuclear activities. On his first trip to Europe after his re-election, President Bush was persuaded by Condoleezza Rice, the new Secretary of State, to move US policy to openly support E3 diplomatic efforts. In part, this shift reflected Washington's broader efforts to mend transatlantic relations after the break-up over Iraq. But Washington also saw a tactical advantage in supporting the European allies: they would be more likely to blame Iran and support stronger sanctions if – as Washington expected – the E3–Iran talks collapsed.

In fact, stronger transatlantic cooperation after 2005 contributed to Iranian disenchantment with the talks, as it demonstrated that Tehran's hopes of dividing the alliance had been misplaced. More importantly, the growing American predicament in Iraq gave Tehran confidence that it could walk away from the E3 talks and end the suspension on enrichment activities. Just as the American victory over Saddam's Iraq in 2003 had created an opening for E3 diplomacy, the mounting evidence of American failure in Iraq doomed the E3 initiative in 2005. Iran took an increasingly strident position in the negotiations, demanding that the Europeans accept Tehran's proposals for a phased enrichment programme or it would be forced to resume some elements of its enrichment activities. Following the election of President Ahmadinejad in June 2005, Iran finally carried out its threat, resuming the conversion of uranium oxide into uranium hexafluoride (UF_6) gas at the Esfahan facility in August.[11]

Although the Bush administration continues to be divided over Iran, the intensifying troubles in Iraq and the growing ascendancy of Secretary of State Rice have driven Washington to place increased emphasis on traditional multilateral diplomacy, which depends, in the first instance, on solid transatlantic cooperation. After the collapse of the E3–Iran talks, the US and E3 worked together to build pressure on Iran to restore the suspension as a condition for resuming international negotiations. In particular, this meant convincing China and Russia to support political pressure and sanctions, although both Beijing and Moscow feared that these measures would damage their bilateral relations with Iran and lead to increased tensions and even war.

Initially, prospects for achieving a strong P5 consensus were uncertain. In September 2005, both Russia and China abstained from an IAEA Board of Governors resolution finding Iran in non-compliance with its safeguards obligations and threatening to refer it to the Security Council if it did not restore the suspension. But when Iran responded by beginning enrichment of UF_6 in January 2006, and rejected Russia's compromise proposal for a joint venture to enrich uranium for Iran on Russian soil, both Russia and China supported an IAEA Board of Governors resolution in February 2006 that finally did refer Iran to the Security Council for action.

Despite some disagreements between the allies on the tactics of their separate and joint approaches to Moscow and Beijing, their eventual success in bringing Russia and China on board, including gaining their support for incremental Security Council sanctions, has been encouraging. As the transatlantic alliance strategy of building a P5 consensus against Iran's activities has gained traction, there seems to be growing confidence in Washington and the E3 capitals that Iranian resistance is wearing down.

From the spring of 2006 to the spring of 2007, the elements for the current strategy fell into place. On 29 March 2006 in New York, the Security Council issued a weak presidential statement calling on Iran to suspend all enrichment-related activities within 30 days. When Iran defied this request, the allies agreed on a new strategy designed to either lure Iran back into negotiations based on suspension or convince Russia and China that stronger UN measures were necessary.

In Vienna on 1 June, the E3+3 agreed on the essential blueprint for the current two-track approach. A generous incentives package was agreed upon, expanding on an E3 offer of August 2005. The US effectively reversed a 27-year-old policy of refusing to deal with Iran by fully endorsing this package, agreeing in principle to join multilateral negotiations (along with the E3, China and Russia), and offering to lift sanctions that had been in place since 1979. The six agreed that these negotiations could only take place on the condition that Iran suspended its enrichment-related and reprocessing activities while they went on. They also agreed upon a confidential comprehensive list of 'measures' (i.e. sanctions) to be applied in the event that Iran failed to comply.

In the year that followed, the Security Council adopted three resolutions, all with the unanimous support of the P5, and all but one with full unanimity. After Iran's rejection of the June offer, Russia and China supported Security Council Resolution 1696 of 31 July 2006, which demanded that Iran 'suspend all enrichment-related and reprocessing activities' by 31 August, and endorsed proposals from the P5 + Germany to seek a negotiated arrangement to confirm the alleged peaceful nature of Iran's nuclear programme. The resolution threatened action under Article 41 of Chapter Seven of the UN Charter if Iran continued its defiance.

Iran did not comply. After months of negotiations among the P5, the Security Council passed Security Council Resolution 1737 (UNSCR 1737) on 23 December 2006, which imposed a 60-day deadline on Iran for the suspension of all enrichment and reprocessing activities as a basis for beginning negotiations, and imposed travel and financial sanctions on a small number of Iranian individuals and entities directly engaged with or providing support for 'sensitive nuclear activities', as well as an embargo on sensitive goods and technologies destined for the Iranian nuclear and ballistic programmes.

The main reason for the delay in achieving P5 consensus on UNSCR 1737 was reluctance on the part of China and especially Russia to impose these sanctions on Iran, but the delay also reflected tactical differences among the Western allies. Emphasising the importance of P5 unity as an instrument for putting political pressure on Tehran, the Europeans were prepared to soften the proposed sanctions in order to win support from Moscow and Beijing. The US was more focused on maintaining stronger sanctions, even if at the cost of Russian abstention. In the end, Washington, choosing to stay on the diplomatic track, made the concessions necessary to maintain P5 consensus.

In fact, the powerful signal sent by a unanimous vote succeeded in affecting the political debate in Tehran. Iranian political leaders, who had reportedly been confident that Russia and China would protect Iran from UN sanctions, were dismayed and angry when Moscow and Beijing supported the resolution. Ahmadinejad's political rivals criticised the president's confrontational approach, and the business community expressed concern that formal and informal sanctions would harm their economic interests. Despite this growing pressure, Iran continued to reject Security Council demands to restore suspension, but the P5 were quick to respond with Resolution 1747 on 23 March 2007, setting another 60-day deadline. The resolution continued the strategy of applying incremental and reversible sanctions. Financial sanctions were extended beyond a few individuals directly involved in nuclear activities to include senior commanders of the Revolutionary Guard and a large Iranian bank, Sepah, thought to be involved in financial transactions for missile-related purchases. In addition, the resolution demanded that Iran halt all weapons exports and called on states to exercise 'restraint' in supplying Iran with heavy weapons, suggesting that future resolutions could impose a full arms embargo if Iran continued to reject Security Council demands. It also called on states and international financial institutions not to provide new grants or loans to Iran except for humanitarian or development purposes, thus deepening Iran's isolation. Finally, the resolution reiterated both the Council's support for the E3+3 offer to begin negotiations with Iran if it suspended its enrichment-related activities, and the principle of UNSCR 1737 that sanctions would be suspended during any talks.

At the same time, the European Union formally adopted sanctions going beyond those of the Security Council, thus signalling both to Washington and to Tehran its determination to pressure Iran. It imposed a visa ban on targeted individuals (whereas the Security Council only called upon states to exercise vigilance and restraint regarding their travel); added a number of individuals and entities to the sanctions list; adopted a formal arms embargo against Tehran; and broadened the embargo on sensitive goods and technologies well beyond the items listed by the Security Council. These measures, which were adopted by the EU Council of Ministers, enhanced the 'informal sanctions' that had already effectively been imposed by banks and other private firms whose own risk assessments had prompted them to minimise business with Iran. French banks, for example, halved their exposure between March 2006 and March 2007. Many UK and continental financial institutions stopped new lending. Export credit guarantees from the largest European countries also diminished, due both to more restrictive government practices and the reduced number of companies seeking guarantees for export deals.

Crunch point

The next year or two will show whether the P5's strategy can succeed. P5 unity may well be put to severe test, whichever direction Tehran takes.

Given the disastrous state of the Iranian economy – inflation and unemployment are skyrocketing, gasoline rationing has been put in place for the first time in decades, the stock market is plummeting – and the additional economic, financial and political havoc that tightened sanctions in the financial sector could play, Tehran may choose to seek some sort of negotiated solution aimed at dividing the international community and retaining key nuclear capabilities. After it has attained a particular threshold – such as the installation of 3,000 centrifuge machines at the underground enrichment plant at Natanz – Tehran may for instance agree to temporarily suspend all or part of its enrichment activities in exchange for the suspension of sanctions and the beginning of negotiations with the E3+3. The Supreme Leader, wishing to increase Iran's manoeuvring room, and fearing the reckless policy of Ahmadinejad, may even succeed in putting a less provocative faction back to the fore.

This scenario would test E3+3 unity. In such negotiations, Iran would seek to retain elements of its enrichment programme under various technical and political constraints, such as additional international inspections or the establishment of an international consortium to own and operate an enrichment facility in Iran. Technically, legally and diplomatically, however, there is no viable alternative to maintaining transatlantic consensus on the key demand that Tehran actually stop all of its enrichment-related activities, reprocessing and heavy-water-related projects, at least for a significant period of time. Technically, any other solution would allow Tehran to continue on its path to a nuclear-weapons capability. Even if significant materials were not covertly diverted from a reduced and stringently inspected enrichment plant, decisive know-how could be, enabling the pursuit of clandestine operations. Legally, the Security Council has made the mandate for full and verified suspension clear in three Chapter Seven resolutions. Diplomatically, the E3+3 could not survive a division on a point as important as this one, and its collapse would mean the end of any prospect of negotiations. However, some members of the E3+3 might be tempted to accept a deal that allowed Iran to retain a restricted enrichment programme, on the basis that this would be a better scenario than Iran with an unrestricted capability. In this view, it is no longer possible to prevent Iran from mastering enrichment technology and the focus of diplomacy must be on preventing it from exercising this capability to produce nuclear weapons.

In another possible scenario, Iran continues to press ahead with its enrichment programme despite international pressure, either because it assesses that it can withstand the pressure, or because internal divisions block a different course. This, too, would put E3+3 unity to the test. In response to Iran's defiance, the Security Council would need to pass additional resolutions to gradually inflict diplomatic isolation and greater economic punishment. Europe's, Russia's and, increasingly, China's substantial trade and financial links to Iran, however, mean that these parties would have to sacrifice hard economic interests in the service of non-proliferation objectives. While the UK and France appear convinced that multilateral diplomacy backed by sanctions is the best option for stopping Iran from developing nuclear weapons and avoiding the risk of war, others in Europe see such escalation as just as likely to lead to war.

The more that the UK and France are able to overcome this resistance within the EU, the easier it will be to persuade Russia and China to continue to support a sanctions strategy – and the easier it will be to keep Washington on board for negotiations. Most importantly, the E3 need to convince Moscow and Beijing that muscular multilateral diplomacy is the most effective means to avoid the danger of war. If Moscow and Beijing conclude that the US is too weak to attack Iran, they will be less inclined to support diplomacy that sacrifices their bilateral economic and political interests with Tehran.

Despite Iraq, however, the possibility of an American military strike against Iranian nuclear facilities is real. If Washington concludes that the Security Council action is not going far enough, fast enough, American faith in non-military means of pressure will ebb. Washington has thus far been patient with the slow pace of international diplomacy, with its emphasis on maintaining P5 unity and gradually increasing pressure, because technical problems have slowed Iran's progress towards a nuclear-weapons capability. If Iran overcomes these technical problems, however, the underlying differences between the US and Europe over military options could surface.

While E3 officials agree that the threat of attack is essential to reinforce diplomacy, the predominant European view today seems to be that the risks of an actual military attack against Iranian nuclear facilities outweigh the potentially limited utility of damaging, but not halting, the programme for an uncertain period of time. In contrast, there is substantial view in the US, and even more so in Israel, that a military attack is worth the risks, even if it only buys a few years. Within the US, this view is not unique to the Bush administration. Given America's special relationship with Israel and its difficult history with Iran – combined with the structural fact that the military option is available – the next administration is also likely to seriously consider air strikes if diplomacy does not succeed. Differences between American and European public opinions are, however, less stark than one might imagine. Polls in 2006 showed that if non-military approaches to the problem failed, 53% of Americans would support military action, compared with 45% of Europeans. Interestingly, a full 54% percent of French respondents said they would support military action were non-military options to fail.[12]

It is difficult to know how the political and diplomatic equation will read at the point that this momentous decision might be taken. Indeed, it will even be difficult to define when a crucial decision point is reached, because Iran's accumulation of enrichment capability, in terms of installing and operating reliable centrifuge machines, is likely to be gradual and incremental. Loose talk today, either in favour of or against a military option whatever the circumstances, is not a good indicator of what will take place at the time of crisis.

Military action against Iran would entail substantial risks. It could be seen to be legitimate – in terms of upholding the international order against Iran's continued defiance of the international community – and would be legal if the Security Council authorised it, as well as politically justified if Iran took some provocative step such as expelling international inspectors or withdrawing from the NPT. Yet legitimacy and legality might well have only a marginal tempering effect on the regional and global blowback that could result. At the same time, ruling out military action under any circumstances seems no more judicious than putting it to the fore. Taking the option off the table reduces the pressure on Iran to change its strategic calculations. Moreover, the day may come when the international community will have nothing but very bad options from which to choose.

Europeans and Americans do not have to agree on how explicitly to brandish the threat of military force – the military threat is an objective reality. The combination of Iran's developing nuclear programme and Ahmadinejad's ranting existential threats against Israel make it impossible to rule out an Israeli response. America, with its intimate political and strategic ties to the Israelis, is unlikely to stop Jerusalem from acting to curb Iran, and may well decide that its own bombing campaign would be preferable because more effective. The prospect of Iranian nuclear ambitions causing military conflict in the not-so-distant future is serious. This prospect should be enough to unite Americans, Europeans, Russians and Chinese around a continued policy of incremental pressure aimed at isolating the Tehran regime, together with a readiness for creative diplomacy to resolve the dispute and end the isolation if and when Iran is ready.

Strengthening the non-proliferation regime

As well as to resolve the Iranian crisis, which poses, along with North Korea, the greatest challenge to the NPT, work is also required to strengthen the non-proliferation regime more broadly. Europeans and Americans are well placed to play a central collaborative role in this endeavour, and have, since the end of the 1990s, been able to secure several significant achievements.

An enduring consciousness of shared interest has largely shielded transatlantic cooperation on non-proliferation, like counter-terrorism, from the clash over Iraq. An example of the resilience of cooperation during this difficult period is the close coordination that allies successfully employed to get Korean Peninsula Energy Development Organisation (KEDO)[13] board members to agree on the stopping of heavy fuel oil shipments to North Korea in 2002, and to suspend the construction of light-water reactors in the following year. The Franco-German interception of a ship bound for North Korea (via China) with aluminium tubes deemed to be for centrifuge production was accomplished in April 2003 at the height of the Iraq crisis. In the aftermath of the crisis, in October 2003, American and European officials worked together to block shipments to Libya's secret nuclear-weapons programme.

The past few years have also seen the emergence of a more pragmatic approach to WMD proliferation among the allies that has brought a much higher level of transatlantic cooperation on the issue than in the early years of the century. Americans have been increasingly able to overcome the aversion to multilateral initiatives that characterised the stark ideological discourse of the first years of the Bush administration, although they still only favour multilateralism of their choosing — i.e., coalitions of the broadly like-minded. Europeans have proved that they are not averse to initiatives that embody ad hoc non-traditional approaches, pursued outside the framework of legally binding negotiated agreements. For both sides, this has been a sea change away from the theological debates of 1999–2001. Two non-proliferation efforts in particular illustrate the change:

- The PSI, which was launched in May 2003, is a good example of the types of ad hoc mechanism that have united Americans and Europeans to solid practical purpose. Eight of its 11 founding members were Europeans, including France and Germany, which at the time of its creation were still in the midst of the worst diplomatic crisis vis-à-vis the United States for decades. The PSI aims to improve coordination among its partner states in intelligence, diplomacy and operational techniques in order to improve their capability to detain, inspect and seize suspect cargo. Due to the classified nature of interdiction operations, it is hard to point to concrete examples of successes, but the initiative is highly acclaimed and probably has a significant deterrent effect. The cooperation it has fostered in intelligence sharing and practising operational responses constitutes a net improvement of collective assets in combating proliferation.[14]
- UN Security Council Resolution 1540 (UNSCR 1540), adopted in April 2004, was co-sponsored by France, the US and the UK, and is an impressive example of multilateralism at work. For the first time since the Iraq crisis, the Security Council was granted a role in counter-proliferation efforts. Adopted a few months after the A.Q. Khan affair came to light, UNSCR 1540 requires that member states adopt *and enforce* domestic legislation to prevent WMD-related activity on their territories, and ensure that they have infrastructure (e.g. border security and physical protection controls[15]) and systems (e.g. export controls) in place to address the threat posed by

non-state actor involvement in WMD proliferation. It also explicitly prohibits states from lending support to non-state actors seeking to acquire WMD or their means of delivery.

Despite this progress, however, there are key areas where political and ideological habits on both sides of the Atlantic indicate something less than full seriousness of purpose. Washington is still carrying some heavy ideological baggage. The stubborn reluctance of the Bush administration to appreciate the merits of the verification of international treaties and commitments continues, long after the notorious scuttling of the verification protocol of the BWC by John Bolton in 2001. The administration has in fact formalised its attitude on this issue, as can be seen in its 2006 proposal for a fissile material cut-off treaty without verification, which could be said to turn Ronald Reagan's famous dictum 'trust but verify' on its head, with a new and rather nonsensical 'don't trust and don't verify'.[16]

Similarly, there remains strong antipathy in Washington towards confidence-building measures (CBMs), even though common sense suggests that most such measures would serve US interests. The Pentagon continues to resist efforts to have the US engage more actively in CBMs in accordance with the BWC, and in the ballistic-missile field. The US undermines the International Code of Conduct on Ballistic Proliferation, for example, by refusing to announce its missile launches.

The Bush administration's most damaging ideological disposition is still its general attitude towards the United Nations. Washington firmly rejects any revival of the UN secretary-general's prerogative to investigate alleged biological-weapons use, which would be a flexible, practical way of involving an impartial and respected third party, thereby laying the groundwork for a strong reaction from the international community should it be needed. The administration has also consistently resisted setting up a mechanism to draw on the expertise and experience of the United Nations Monitoring, Verification and Inspection Commission (UNMOVIC) and United Nations Special Commission inspection teams. This is unwise. Almost a decade of inspections in Iraq not only effectively disarmed the country, but also developed a new, far more integrated approach to verification that could prove very useful in the future. This approach encourages cross-fertilisation between separate fields of expertise (for example, the pooling of nuclear- and ballistic-missile expertise to deal with the issue of suspected weaponisation activities); and makes use of skills and knowledge that are not specific to any individual field of proliferation, but that help to achieve verification goals in all of them. Such skills include interviewing techniques, documentary analysis, information-technology forensic techniques, and analysis of the dynamics of procurement networks. In prevailing upon the Security Council to terminate UNMOVIC's mandate without any follow-up, the Bush administration appears willing to see all of this expertise lost, for reasons that seem ideological rather than practical.

Antipathy to the UN could also, potentially, damage global defences against biological terrorism. The World Health Organisation (WHO) is one of the first lines of defence against both natural pandemic disease and biological terror, which might be indistinguishable in their early stages. But, as biological terrorism expert Christopher Chyba has written, the WHO's 'international disease surveillance system is chronically underfunded and has too many geographical holes'.[17] There is anecdotal evidence that US congressional hostility to UN agencies had contributed to that under-funding.[18]

The European problem is not so much ideological as political – a matter of coherence and seriousness in implementing declared policies. 'Effective multilateralism' is a good slogan. But if it is indeed to be a guiding prin-ciple of European foreign policy, the EU needs to be more willing to put into practice the official sanctions associated with non-compliance with international agreements. In its December 2003 *Strategy Against the Proliferation of Weapons of Mass Destruction*,[19] the EU laid out its plan to put its considerable economic and commercial power to the service of non-proliferation goals by inserting a 'conditionality clause' into all its future commercial agreements. The clause would make respect for non-proliferation commitments a key element of any agreement, with a breach of these commitments initiating a process that could ultimately lead to the suspension of the agreement. For this plan to be effective, it is important that the EU succeeds in including the clause in its agreements with *all* countries, including larger ones with political weight, such as India. It is equally important that, when faced with non-compliance, the EU makes sure to actually impose the associated sanctions.

Another area where Europeans can progress in ensuring that they contribute effectively to non-proliferation efforts is in the G8 Global Partnership Against the Spread of WMD.[20] Despite several success-ful Cooperative Threat Reduction programmes since the collapse of the Soviet Union, the security of Russian nuclear facilities and materi-als remains uneven, and, as a consequence, Russia remains a potential source of nuclear materials for terrorists. Europeans cannot afford to contribute as little as they currently do to threat reduction in the former Soviet Union. It will also be easier to challenge Russia on its own poor implementation of its commitments if there is enough money to contribute to Russian efforts in this area. Although relations with Russia are already difficult for a host of reasons unrelated to proliferation, Europeans and Americans need in addition to find ways to engage with Moscow on lingering suspicions over Russian activities in the field of biological weapons. The reaction from Moscow will no doubt be harsh, but seriousness about international obligations and commitments requires keeping this issue on the agenda.

The proliferation phenomenon has changed over the past decade, and the transatlantic response to it must adapt accordingly. We have seen in a very short time span the emergence of a new type of terrorist organisation that openly strives to acquire and use nuclear and possibly biological and chemical weapons against the West, and the ease with which individuals can harness the power of criminal networks to buy the most sensitive nuclear technologies has become equally apparent. As well as dealing with 'classic' threats from state weapons projects and state non-compliance on WMD issues, such as the threats posed by North Korea and Iran, Europeans and Americans must also be in a position to better deal with weapons-trafficking networks, hostile non-state actors and the prospect of WMD terrorism. Considerable adaptation to the new reality has already taken place – witness the growing, and increasingly successful efforts to counter proliferation financing – but more is needed.

With this challenge in mind, Europe and the United States can make a strong contribution to their own security, and to international order, by focusing in the coming years on the following key projects:

- *Implementing and helping others to implement UNSCR 1540.* To assist in the implementation of this important and innovative resolution, the Security Council established a committee to receive and analyse states' reports on steps they have taken to meet their obligations. However, the committee does not have the mandate or resources to verify reports, and many states have yet to meet the minimal reporting requirements. There are also no common standards for the export controls required by the resolution. Europeans and Americans should find a way to provide for verification, and set standards for export controls. Furthermore, they need to focus on providing the necessary assistance to states that do not have the capabilities to fully meet their resolution commitments alone, while coaxing along those for whom the main problem is not capacity but will.

- *Coordinating to develop strategies and resources for handling the medical, economic, social, political and diplomatic consequences of a terrorist WMD attack.* The few transatlantic tabletop exercises that have been done in the past few years (*Black Dawn* in 2004 dealt with a nuclear attack in Brussels, the scenario for *Atlantic Storm* in 2005 was a terrorist-induced epidemic of an infectious disease affecting transatlantic interests) have given participants a taste of what may lie ahead, and of how inadequate preparations are. Given the near certainty of a mass-casualty WMD attack in the coming decade, it is imperative that more funds and expertise are focused on contingency planning.

The NPT's fragility

The most important and most threatened international barrier against the diffusion of nuclear technologies and materials is the four-decade-old Nuclear Non-Proliferation Treaty. The NPT is threatened both by the resourcefulness and determination of aspiring nuclear powers, and by a worrying lack of faith in the NPT regime on the part of its original signatories. There are three categories of measure that would make the treaty more effective – securing the nuclear fuel cycle, deterring withdrawal from the treaty and dealing with non-compliance – but its long-term viability also requires a restoration of this faith.

- *Securing the nuclear fuel cycle.* For states and terrorists, the biggest obstacle to achieving a nuclear-weapons capability is the difficulty of acquiring sufficient fissile material. Enrichment-related and reprocessing technologies are therefore particularly dangerous. Their transfer needs to be subject to more stringent rules than other nuclear goods. At the same time, however, there is a growing recognition that increased use of nuclear energy is an important item on the menu of measures needed to combat climate change. Consequently, access to nuclear-fuel services will be vital for the increasing number of states that will embark on nuclear-energy programmes in the coming years. Europeans and Americans must take the lead, in the G8, the Nuclear Suppliers' Group (NSG) and the IAEA, to resolve this dilemma. All NSG members but one support the approach of using commonly agreed criteria to regulate the export of the most sensitive technologies. The exception is the United States, which advocates a blanket prohibition on these exports.[21] Such a prohibition would in principle be the most effective measure, but it is politically untenable. It does not have the backing of a single other member of the G8 or NSG.

Moreover, if a blanket prohibition were put in place this would seem to legitimate Iran's portrayal to the Non-Aligned Movement of its nuclear defiance as a heroic stand against the arrogant West; a defence of the 'nuclear rights' of the nuclear have-nots.

Partly as a way of responding to this claim, a number of initiatives for multilateral fuel assurances have been put forward. The proposal with the broadest support was offered in June 2006 by six supplier states (US, Russia, Germany, France, Netherlands, UK).[22] National proposals have also been put forward by the United States, Germany and Russia, and various international organisations have also submitted plans. Whichever arrangement, if any, is chosen, it must serve the political function of reassuring states that they can meet their legitimate, peaceful needs without developing national fuel cycle capabilities.

- *Deterring withdrawal from the NPT.* Under international law, a state that withdraws from the NPT, invoking its rights under Article Ten, remains responsible for violations committed while it was still a party to the treaty. The problem therefore is not, as is sometimes suggested, that there is a loophole in the NPT that would allow a state party to benefit from nuclear cooperation and then withdraw in order to use legally acquired goods for non-peaceful purposes. It is rather how to compel compliance when there are violations and, more broadly, how to make the political and diplomatic costs of withdrawal from the NPT prohibitive. Drawing on lessons from North Korea's announcement of its withdrawal from the treaty in 2003, France put forward proposals on how to deter withdrawal in spring 2004. These gained broader support, and the EU tabled a paper on the subject for the 2005 NPT Review Conference. The United States made its own proposals at the 2007 Preparatory Committee for the 2010 Review Conference.

  In essence, all these proposals suggest that a state that withdraws should no longer be able to make use of any nuclear materials, facilities, equipment or technologies acquired from a third country before its withdrawal. Such facilities, equipment and nuclear material should be returned to the supplying state, frozen or dismantled under international verification. Mohamed ElBaradei's former deputy in charge of safeguards, Pierre Goldschmidt, has in addition proposed that the Security Council should adopt, under Chapter Seven of the UN Charter, a generic resolution to the effect that if a state withdraws from the treaty after being found in non-compliance by the IAEA, then such a withdrawal would constitute a threat to international peace and security.[23]

- *Responding to non-compliance.* As the North Korean and Iranian cases show, an effective Security Council response to non-compliance cannot be taken for granted. In the case of North Korea, during both the 1993–94 and 2002–03 crises, the Security Council was prevented from acting by the position of China. Only after Pyongyang tested ballistic missiles in July 2006 and then detonated a nuclear device in October 2006 did the Security Council take action. The response had been too late to prevent North Korean from acquiring nuclear weapons. In the case of Iran, the case for non-compliance was essentially established by the IAEA Board of Governors as early as September 2003; yet the dossier was formally referred to the Security Council only in a two-stage process in September 2005 and February 2006, after Iran had started enriching UF_6. The advantages of a generic country-neutral resolution for dealing with such cases have been argued persuasively by Goldschmidt.[24] In essence, the Security Council should adopt a generic and legally binding resolution containing a standard set of actions to be taken when countries have been found by the IAEA to be in non-compliance, including the provision to the IAEA of additional verification rights and the temporary suspension of sensitive fuel cycle activities.

*   *   *

The purpose of this paper is to focus on pragmatic transatlantic cooperation without necessarily engaging deeper philosophical disputes between the US and Europe. In the case of proliferation, however, there may well be a philosophical disagreement that cannot be ignored for much longer. It concerns, in effect, whether the NPT is to be considered a critical barrier to proliferation, and whether the basic regime is in danger or can be taken for granted.

Like many multilateral treaties, the NPT is the expression of a norm that is understood to have some traction in its own right, independent of the specific penalties for specific violators the treaty can impose. Europeans are perhaps more likely than Americans to have faith that treaties can indeed exert such power, just as they are more likely to be dedicated to the norms of international order as values and ends in themselves. Recent US administrations – not just the current one – have been more likely to argue that it is rather the nature of the regimes – hostile or friendly, despotic or democratic – that counts.

But imagining that the NPT has no inherent, normative power of its own can lead to policies that allow it to wither. The NPT regime is inherently weak because it is deeply counter-intuitive. The notion that five (or six or eight) states in the world have a natural and exclusive right to possess mankind's most powerful weapons is one that naturally offends fundamental conceptions of reciprocity, fairness and sovereign equality. Thus, the basic bargain of the NPT was that the vast majority of the world's sovereign states would forswear the development of these weapons in return for a commitment from the five nuclear-weapons states to eventual disarmament. In the middle of a Cold War arms race, the disarmament pledge could be discounted as utopian. Almost 20 years after the Cold War, disarmament remains a faraway if not utopian goal – but the patience of nuclear have-nots can be expected to wear thin.

Consideration of this problem should be enough to convince transatlantic allies – who account for three of the NPT's five nuclear-weapons states – to agree on a menu of disarmament ideas they could offer to the Non-Aligned Movement and other nuclear have-nots, in exchange for their cooperation in measures to strengthen the NPT, as explored above. This would of course only make sense if the allies were to get Russian and, in particular, Chinese support as well. Part of the package should be a serious proposal for substantial further cuts in US and Russian nuclear forces and time-bound nuclear test and fissile-material production moratoriums.

The Bush administration may not be interested, and there is reason to be sceptical that a grand bargain can be reached with the Non-Aligned Movement in any event. But a new US administration will take office in 2009 and another NPT Review Conference is scheduled for 2010. There were various reasons for the undoubted failure of the 2005 conference – but perceived US lack of interest was certainly one of them, along with Egyptian and Iranian obstructionism. Expert and policymaking communities on both sides of the Atlantic should begin now to consider and debate a comprehensive package that could be put forth and defended in three years' time.

CHAPTER THREE

State Failure, State-building and Democratic Change

In the decade before 11 September, there were plenty of failed and failing states around the world, but very little clarity among transatlantic powers about their strategic interests and moral responsibilities for rescuing them.[1] The absence of the strategic focus that had been provided by the East–West struggle was keenly felt, and could be seen in the confusion of Western responses to state breakdown and civil war in Afghanistan, Rwanda, Yugoslavia, Zaire/DRC, Angola, Liberia, Sierra Leone and former Soviet republics in Central Asia and the Caucasus – to name a few. Some of these civil conflicts, for example those in Afghanistan and Angola, were continuations of Cold War proxy wars that maintained their deadly momentum long after the superpower patrons had lost interest. Others – in Yugoslavia and some former Soviet republics – were the consequence of the collapse of the last multinational empires and federations. Since both these groups of wars fitted into the category of unfinished business from the twentieth century's cold and world wars, it was possible initially to hope that the local carnage of the 1990s was a kind of final, knock-on nightmare – terrible, but temporary.

This interpretation fit the general optimism engendered by the peaceful conclusion of the Cold War. A theory of benign globalisation suggested that these poor and conflict-ridden regions eventually would be swept up in the tide of global progress and peaceful development. If this was the long-term prospect, then it could be argued that the main responsibility of the powerful, advanced and wealthy states was to promote the requisite global conditions – free trade, freer movement of human and financial capital, secure sources of energy, minimal interstate conflict – while attending in the short term to the humanitarian consequences of local conflicts.

As the 1990s dragged on, however, the multiplicity, obduracy, brutality and sheer anarchy of such conflicts pointed to a darker interpretation – that a strong state and competent governance were preconditions for peaceful progress, but that these preconditions were not natural or perhaps even attainable in many places. The concept of 'failed states' entered the common discourse of international relations, together with the overriding question: what, if anything, could and would be done to resurrect them?

This question became entangled with two other emerging aspects of the post-Cold War international system. Increasing recognition of the primacy of American power was combined, perhaps inevitably, with increasing concern about the steadfastness of the United States' exercise of its preponderant power. In relation to the problem of failed states, the focus on the United States came as alternative solutions were, or appeared to be, discredited. With the end of the Cold War, new expectations and great demands were placed on the United Nations as an organisation, and although it performed admirably in many places, some notable failures – Somalia, Rwanda and Yugoslavia – underscored its material and cultural limits. Europe, both its institutions and its major powers, proved inadequate to the overriding challenge it faced in the dissolution of Yugoslavia. Indeed, the notion of America as the 'indispensable' power owed much to the way it was drawn into the role of leading peacemaker to pick up the pieces of Yugoslavia's collapse, first in Bosnia, then in Kosovo.[2] Yet looking at the 1990s as a whole, the American record in dealing with the most horrific consequences of state failure was uneven at best. Its flight from Somalia propagated the new conventional wisdom that a ruthless warlord need only fill a few body bags to dispatch the last remaining superpower. Haunted, clearly, by that experience, the US not only baulked itself but also stymied any effective UN Security Council action to halt the Rwandan genocide. In Haiti, the US role was more honourable and marginally more successful – but critics noted that the motivating interest was in large measure the prospect of more waves of Haitian refugees. And even in Yugoslavia, where the US led its NATO allies in performing effectively in the end, initial American diffidence played a major role in stalling an effective Western response until much of the damage – especially in Bosnia – had already been done.

Such was the background to one of the few debates in the 2000 US presidential contest devoted to foreign policy. The George W. Bush campaign accused the Clinton administration of having lost America's strategic focus, squandering its military assets and energy on peacekeeping and 'nation-building' exercises in places far removed from the United States' vital interests. Vice President Al Gore responded with a spirited defence of such engagements (the salient issue at the time was the Balkans deployments); he noted that nation-building in Germany and Japan had been key ingredients in America's post-war and Cold War foreign policy triumphs.

It might be imagined that the terrorist attacks of 11 September would have settled this particular debate. Osama bin Laden and al-Qaeda had in effect hijacked the failed states of Sudan and then Afghanistan for their base of operations. Since the enormity of the threat from al-Qaeda was now firmly established, it would seem to follow that the world community, and not least the United States, could no longer tolerate the scourge of failed states – for strategic as much as for moral reasons. And indeed, the strategic threat posed by failed states was highlighted in the Bush administration's 2002 National Security Strategy, which stated on page one that 'America is now threatened less by conquering states than we are by failing ones'. The European Union's security strategy document of 2003 makes a similar assertion.[3] This apparent lesson was underscored by President Bush's promise to Afghanistan, at the outset of the US war there, that the United States would not abandon the country again to its post-war fate. Implicit in this promise was the idea that American neglect of the country in the decade after the Soviet withdrawal had been a catastrophic mistake.

And yet – whatever the merits in principle of the argument that state failure around the globe is intolerable to the international conscience and international security – the practical problem of strategic choice will not easily go away. In the best of all plausible worlds, some failed states would be the (presumably fortunate) objects of international ministration, and some would not. The criteria for choosing who gets pulled into the lifeboat are murky – certainly in moral terms but also in terms of national interest. One serious attempt to lay out such strategic-choice criteria came in the mid 1990s from a team of scholars led by Yale historian Paul Kennedy. They drew up a list of 'pivotal states' that the Western and international communities could not afford to let fail.[4] The inherent flaw in any such attempt at list-making is easy to see: it is unlikely that Afghanistan, before 11 September, would have made the shortlist.

The six most dangerous places in the world

At the forefront of current international anxiety are six especially frightening candidates for state failure: Iraq, Palestine, Lebanon, Afghanistan,

Pakistan and North Korea. These are not in every case the most pressing humanitarian crises that the world faces. The fates of only a couple of them – Afghanistan and, more tangentially, Palestine and Lebanon, are likely to depend to any large extent on effective transatlantic cooperation. They are also six very different cases. Iraq is already sinking into civil war. Palestine's importance derives in particular from the emotive power that its thwarted quest for statehood exerts over the Arab and Islamic worlds. Lebanon provides heartbreaking evidence that arrangements to reconcile competing communities in the Middle East are dangerously fragile. Afghanistan is a failed state that NATO is trying to re-establish to a condition of minimal viability. Pakistan can best be understood as a failed democracy in which a more or less benign military ruler seems to be the only obvious bulwark against broader state failure. North Korea is an isolated kingdom of surreal Stalinism whose people are tightly regimented and nearly starving, and whose rulers have a nuclear capability and a record of selling anything they can get their hands on to anyone willing to buy.

What these six nations have in common is that they are not only precarious, but central to global and transatlantic security. Most of them are plausible candidates for civil war. Five of them are at the centre of the intensifying crisis of relations between the Islamic world and the West. Two of the six are prospective embodiments of what some fear could be the twenty-first century's recurring nightmare – failed states with terrorist connections and nuclear weapons.

Iraq

The American-led war for regime change in Iraq has converted that country from vicious tyranny to near anarchy. It is not clear that international security or even the condition of the Iraqi people have improved as a result. What is clear, as of mid 2007, is that American and Coalition military forces are not winning in Iraq, and that avoiding the worst kind of defeat requires a strategy that matches realistic goals with the resources to reach them.

There is little *Schadenfreude* in Europe over America's predicament in Iraq. It is possible that initially, as Brookings Institution scholar Philip Gordon has suggested, some European opponents feared that an early and dramatic success in Iraq might embolden the United States for similar adventures elsewhere.[5] But the emboldening effects of easy and dramatic success are not quite the current problem. The wider effects of continued failure in Iraq would affect Europeans and Americans alike.

The November 2006 US midterm elections were seen in large measure as a referendum on the Bush administration's handling of Iraq. The decisive Republican defeat in both the Senate and House of Representatives showed a palpable public desire to reassess the American strategy. The Iraq Study Group, co-chaired by former Secretary of State James Baker and former Democratic Congressman Lee Hamilton, issued its report in late 2006, urging the administration to sharply curtail its ambitions in Iraq. The president's nomination of a member of this group, former CIA Director Robert Gates, to replace Donald Rumsfeld as Secretary of Defense indicated a possibility that its recommendations might perhaps be implemented.

However, President Bush decided instead on a minor escalation – a 'surge' of some 30,000 extra troops to try once again to secure Baghdad, using counter-insurgency principles as articulated and practised by General David Petraeus, the new commander of Coalition forces. A few months into the 'surge', the success of these principles was, on a micro level, demonstrable – it was possible to provide some greater measure of human security and bring, here or there, a Baghdad neighbourhood back to life. Yet successes such as these are probably unsustainable in the long run: both Iraqi and American publics have lost faith in US capabilities (and, in the case of some Iraqis, in US intentions); there simply are not sufficient US troops to provide real security for the whole country; the most violent of the Shia militias engaged in sectarian horrors have probably been laying low rather than giving up; the Iraqi forces being trained by Americans are of uncertain loyalty and often, especially in the case of police, parties to the civil war; and there is, in effect, no real Iraqi government with the competence, capacity or will to embody the kind of compact among the country's three main communities that might quell the civil war As IISS Senior Fellow Toby Dodge has observed, 'Even if there was the political will, in a country dominated by a collapsed state, the ability of the government to build up its capacity across a sustained geographical area is very limited'.[6]

Just before the US midterms, Peter Beinart of *The New Republic* laid out a useful taxonomy of the options that are, in theory, still available.[7] Assessing their practical feasibility, however, is a depressing exercise. One category involves significantly more troops, or at least significantly improved military strategy, to improve human security and thereby alleviate the terror that is driving Iraqis into the arms of murderous sectarian 'protectors'. The second category is a cluster of what Beinart calls 'Hail Mary' options – political and constitutional fixes that might satisfy sufficient shares of both the Sunni and Shia populations to reduce the clout of insurgents and militias. The third category encompasses various versions of an American retreat.

The problem with the first category is that there is self-evidently no stomach in American politics for sending significantly more troops; the time that a strained US military would require to recruit, train and deploy them is outside the time frame for saving the situation anyway; and, as the 'surge' demonstrates, improved military strategies are already being implemented with effects on the overall level of violence that may not be sustainable. The problem with the second is that sectarian terror and fear-mongering have reached a level where the kind of basic national compact that might have saved Iraqi society two or three years ago is considerably less viable today. This is one reason that the 'Hail Mary' options include a number of plans for varying degrees of federalism or partition, such as put forward by Senator Joseph Biden, former Council on Foreign Relations President Leslie Gelb, and former US Ambassador to Croatia Peter Galbraith. Galbraith, for one, insists that his is not a plan for America to partition Iraq, but rather a recognition that the Iraqis are already doing it themselves.[8] The counter-argument to this is that the urban mixing of Iraq's populations makes full partition a nightmare that should not yet be accepted.[9]

In late 2006, *Newsweek* editor Fareed Zakaria sketched out an initiative whereby the country's Shia leadership might convincingly offer disaffected Sunnis positions of political responsibility and economic empowerment, a guaranteed share of oil revenues, safety from militia death squads, and amnesty for insurgents and militias alike.[10] The Shia-dominated government of Prime Minister Nuri al-Maliki continues to resist making such an offer. Thus, there is an inexorable logic to flirting with the third category of options: for US withdrawal. The prospect of US troops leaving could be leveraged, argued Zakaria, for the purpose of concentrating Iraqi leaders' minds on what they need to do to escape civil war. If they are still unable to make a compact that might ease sectarian strife, the US should be ready to cut troop levels from 144,000 to about 60,000:

> a rapid reaction force to secure certain core interests … first, to prevent Anbar province from being taken over by Qaeda-style jihadist groups that would use it as a base for global terrorism; second, to ensure that the Kurdish region retains its autonomy; third, to prevent or at least contain massive sectarian violence in Iraq, as both a humanitarian and a security issue.[11]

Many Democratic critics of the war, including leading presidential candidates such as Hillary Clinton and Barack Obama, anticipate leaving a smaller residual force for such purposes. Yet it is reasonable to question whether a much smaller force can accomplish what higher troop levels cannot accomplish. Steven Simon, Council on Foreign Relations senior fellow and a member of the IISS transatlantic relations steering group, argues that the key issue is for the United States to begin to plan its near total withdrawal, to avoid the worst case of an ignominious, panicky rout:

> The time has come to acknowledge that the United States must fundamentally recast its commitment to Iraq. It must do so without any illusions that there are unexplored or magic fixes, whether diplomatic or military. Some disasters are irretrievable. Having staked its prestige on the intervention and failed to achieve many of its objectives, the United States will certainly pay a price for military disengagement from Iraq. But if the United States manages its departure from Iraq carefully, it will not have lost everything. Rather, the United States will have preserved the opportunity to recover vital assets that its campaign in Iraq has imperilled: diplomatic initiative, global reputation, and the well-being and political utility of its ground forces.[12]

What these net assessments of real possibilities have in common is that they are mostly grim. This grim reality must, in turn, set limits on what can be expected of the transatlantic alliance. The hard truth is that while Iraq can continue to hurt the alliance, there is very little that the alliance can do to help Iraq. Europe has nothing substantial to offer in terms of extra military capacity. This is not surprising: the US administration itself was either unable or unwilling to commit the numbers of troops, probably in the order of half a million, that might have secured the country, even in the early months when the US electorate supported the invasion.[13] That support has now dissipated. In the case of countries such as Germany and France, where electorates overwhelmingly opposed the invasion from the start, it is hardly realistic to imagine governments committing troops to a military occupation that is visibly failing.

What European allies *can* do is relieve the pressure elsewhere. The military and civilian effort in Afghanistan, discussed below, is NATO's biggest current challenge. Likewise, the Europeans' capacity and willingness to send peacekeepers to Lebanon, where they are needed to prevent a resumption of war between Israel and Hizbullah, serves, inter alia, the interests of an overstretched United States that cannot afford extended conflagration in the Middle East (notwithstanding the illusions of some in Washington that Israel's Lebanon War of summer 2006 was a necessary campaign in the West's incipient war with Iran[14]). There are sure to be more such peacekeeping emergencies requiring military capacity that only Europeans can provide.

The other area where European allies can make a modest but still significant contribution is to diplomacy. This will require a shift in American thinking about the regional dimensions of the Iraq War. Veteran US diplomat and member of the IISS steering group James Dobbins has put it succinctly: the US cannot expect to stabilise Iraq if it is simultaneously set on *de*stabilising Iraq's neighbours with a policy of regime change in Iran and Syria. Iraq has countless pressure points vulnerable to Iranian and Syrian interests. Iran in particular exerts powerful political influence over its Shia-dominated neighbour, and a more successful Western policy on Iraq has to begin by acknowledging this reality. Talks involving Iran and Syria will be no panacea for the Iraq crisis, but it cannot be resolved without them. As Dobbins also notes, to end the Bosnian war it proved necessary to engage the help of Slobodan Milosevic and Franjo Tudjman, men who shared responsibility for genocide there. Compromise with Syrian and Iranian regimes will likewise be necessary. The United States may have a weak hand, but it may be able to leverage Syria and Iran's real interest in avoiding the blowback into their own territories of a regional catastrophe.

There are signs that the US is beginning to recognise this necessity. The Bush administration rejected the Iraq Study Group's appeal for talks with Syria and Iran – and then proceeded, within the next seven months, to conduct official meetings with both. In May 2007 US Ambassador to Iraq Ryan Crocker sat down with his Iranian counterpart to discuss measures to stabilise Iraq, and more such meetings were planned.[15] However reluctantly undertaken, these moves, together with the Iraq Study Group's proposal for convening a regional conference, indicate that an American consensus is moving closer to the Europeans' somewhat greater emphasis on diplomacy.[16]

There are a variety of possible vehicles for diplomacy on Iraq. 'Contact groups' of interested powers have been more or less effective in coping with other conflicts. The 'Quartet' of the US, EU, UN and Russia oversaw the 'roadmap' for peace between Israelis and Palestinians – though without, it must be said, getting very far down the road. More successfully, the diplomacy that ended Bosnia's civil war was conducted under the rubric of a formal contact group comprising the US, France, Germany, the UK and Russia.

A similar contact group for Iraq might have been resisted in the past, by Americans because they were determined to dominate Iraq policy, and by

Europeans precisely because they feared that any such mechanism would be used as a multilateral cover for US domination. But the United States is no longer able to dominate events in Iraq, if it ever was. It should enlist the EU's help in organising a regional security forum to aid the integration of Iraq into regional structures, with the aim of committing the country's neighbours to its stabilisation. Such a forum would be roughly the same as the 'Iraq International Support Group' proposed by the Iraq Study Group.[17] Once established, the remit of the forum might be expanded to include other major security issues, such as terrorism and proliferation, on the model of the Arms Control and Regional Security initiative of the Madrid Process following the 1991 Gulf War.

Very clearly, such mechanisms are not magic fixes for recovering the Iraq disaster. Iran and Syria have too strong motives to keep bleeding America in Iraq (barring inconceivable US concessions on nuclear weapons and Lebanon respectively), and even if Tehran and Damascus stopped supporting various factions in Iraq, it is probably too late to reverse the civil war and prevent de facto partition when the US inevitably leaves. As the US starts to draw down its forces, however, the balance of leverage and interest may shift gradually against Iran in particular, since Iran has no real interest in chaos on its borders. With a real prospect of American withdrawal, a regional security forum might help to minimise and manage the regional consequences.

Palestine and Lebanon
A valuable contribution of the Iraq Study Group was that a commission of nine American elder statesmen and one woman stated clearly that the US should be attentive to the links between the unresolved Israel–Palestine conflict and the crisis in Iraq – and, indeed, instability in the broader Middle East. In the past it has been difficult for American leaders to acknowledge the connections, but the two occupations – Iraq and Palestine – are in fact closely connected in the thinking of Arabs.

These connections have long been argued by Europeans, and disagreement about the centrality of Israel–Palestine to other problems in the Middle East has been a key cause of transatlantic disaffection. The disaffection continues, even though official US and European policies have converged considerably.

In 2002, the creation of the Quartet gave the Europeans the seat at the Middle East table that they had previously been denied. Within this framework, the United States and the EU, represented by Javier Solana, agreed in September 2002 on a 'roadmap for peace'. Formally released on 30 April 2003, it has undergone many revisions in the interim. The roadmap and subsequent adjustments to it were, in part, the Bush administration's response to the Europeans' appeal, in the strained run-up to and aftermath of the Iraq invasion, to the US to devote more attention to Israel–Palestine. Tony Blair in particular made the issue a personal priority and central theme of his July 2003 and November 2004 visits to Washington. Consistent, however, with its argument that Israel–Palestine was peripheral to the war on terror, the Bush administration pressed the plan only tepidly, and pinned its best hope of improving the situation on the policies of the Sharon government, especially its unilateral withdrawal from Gaza. Yet, European discontent over this posture[18] notwithstanding, the new transatlantic consensus as embodied by the roadmap has survived to the present.

Consensus is not always an unalloyed good. The roadmap has not been implemented in any significant measure. To be fair, it was conceived at time when any confidence that might have existed between Israelis and Palestinians had been shattered by two years of popular uprising on the Palestinian side (the second intifada), horrendous terrorist attacks by Palestinian extremists, and large-scale and often indiscriminate military operations by the Israelis in response. The Israeli government under Ariel Sharon declared that Palestinian Authority President Yassir Arafat was an accomplice of terrorists, and in consequence effectively refused to engage with the Palestinian Authority. Israel's policy of unilateral 'separation' – which it stated it would pursue on its own terms for as long as no valid Palestinian 'partner for peace' emerged – understandably appealed to an Israeli public traumatised by the terrorism wave of 2000–02. The policy was implemented in the September 2005 withdrawal from Gaza, and the beginning of the construction of the highly controversial West Bank 'separation barrier' (of which 500 kilometres of the 700km approved by the Israeli government have been built so far).

This cascade of negative circumstances made the resumption of a peace process an unlikely prospect in the years that followed the promulgation of the roadmap, and the situation was further complicated by three developments in 2006. First, the victory of Hamas in Palestinian legislative elections in January led to the formation of a Hamas-dominated cabinet under Prime Minister Ismail Haniyeh. Then in late June Palestinian operatives abducted an Israeli soldier and killed two others, and Israel temporarily reoccupied part of Gaza and conducted intensive military operations in response. Hizbullah's subsequent kidnapping of two Israeli soldiers and killing of several others then provoked the Israeli air and ground campaign in Lebanon of July–August 2006.

The roadmap was rickety even without the burden of these crises. It lacked a monitoring mechanism to assess compliance,[19] which allowed each party, and the Sharon government in particular, to claim that nothing had been accomplished by the other. Like the Oslo agreement before it, the roadmap offered only the most gradual progress, and no indication of the principles and parameters that should guide the resolution of final status, presenting the Palestinians with few new incentives for the steps required of them. This was a time when the Palestinian public had come to regard the entire process begun in 1993 as a series of political concessions on their part with no prospect of an honourable final agreement in sight, while their situation on the ground steadily deteriorated.

The Europeans have essentially deferred to the American and Israeli position that the main problem with the peace process is the lack of a suitable interlocutor on the Palestinian side. They joined the Americans in refusing to deal with the Hamas majority government and in suspending direct aid to the Palestinian Authority until three conditions were satisfied: a commitment to non-violence, recognition of Israel, and acceptance of the previous commitments and obligations of the PA, including to the roadmap. This position was principled rather than pragmatic, since it held the new Palestinian government accountable for what it said rather than for what it did, in contrast to the 'performance-based' roadmap. Moreover, the position lacked the very symmetry of obligations that the roadmap had been designed to supply.

From a European perspective, the bitter irony is that Europe was excluded from the peace process while it functioned, then welcomed into it, via the Quartet, only to preside over its demise. The transatlantic partners have been more or less passive witnesses to this demise. The 18 months following Hamas's electoral victory were marked by street fighting between PA security forces, dominated by Fatah, and Hamas militants. Truces between the two factions were generally short-lived. The members of the Quartet, with varying degrees of enthusiasm, continued the policy of isolating the Hamas government even after Hamas became the senior partner in a Saudi-brokered unity government in March 2007. The Bush administration went so far as to actively encourage what was effectively a coup attempt by Fatah security forces against Hamas.[20] This coup attempt failed, and a major armed showdown between the two factions led to Hamas ejecting Fatah from the Gaza Strip in June 2007. The consequence, at the time of this writing, was effectively two separate Palestinian entities – Hamas-dominated in Gaza; Fatah-dominated in the West Bank – both in circumstances of incipient state failure.

At this point, the Americans and the Europeans need to take more seriously both their partnership and the issue at hand. This requires less ambitious objectives and more seriousness in pursuing them. The task today is not to create the pretence of a functioning peace process, when the conditions for it are clearly missing, but to keep open the option of an eventual two-state solution. This more limited, but in fact highly demanding, objective will require a common agenda that may appear to be directed against the current policies of the Israeli government, since many of the facts on the ground which threaten to foreclose the two-state option tend to come from the Israeli side. These include continued settlement expansion and the path of the separation barrier that encompasses unjustifiable settlements and virtually imprisons some Palestinian communities. Palestinian responsibilities are also clear: terrorism has played a decisive role in destroying the peace process, creating a profound disbelief within Israel in the possibility of achieving a genuine peace with any future Palestinian state.

It is a truism that only the Palestinians and Israelis themselves can restore some measure of mutual confidence and resume the peace process. It is also clear, however, that outside powers need to provide a framework that would make this restoration possible. This reality presents Americans and Europeans with some immediate and some longer-term tasks. Firstly, they need to find a formula for bringing relief to the Palestinians. Rigid rejection of a Hamas-led government's legitimacy – on the reasonable basis that it engages in terrorism and refuses to acknowledge Israel's right to exist – is right in principle and wrong in most practical applications. It is in nobody's interest but Hamas' for the West to be blamed for the further breakdown of Palestinian society. The idea of a 'West Bank first' policy – effectively 'rewarding' the areas under Fatah control while allowing Hamas-run Gaza to fester in misery – will only compound the Quartet's previous errors.[21] The EU may be ready to move in the opposite direction, with an aid agenda that recognises the necessity of rescuing Gaza and, consequently, the need for some limited dealings with Hamas. (Indeed, there was an element of constructive hypocrisy to the EU's earlier stance, since its aid to Palestine actually increased in 2006 compared to 2005, despite the election of a Hamas government.)

Secondly, they should independently monitor and report the performance of both sides. From settlement activities to the renunciation of violence, it is essential that independent reliable information is made available to societies that are routinely presented with factually dubious descriptions of the horrendous intentions and behaviour of the other side. It may turn out to be far more important to report accurately on the degree to which the Hamas government has observed its unilaterally proclaimed truce than to extract from it a blanket statement of renunciation of violence.

Thirdly, the outside parties have an important role to play in reversing the prevailing incapacity on both sides to believe that peace is possible. Americans and Europeans can do this together by outlining their common view of the desired end state. It is true that details of final status must be negotiated by the contending parties. Yet any viable and fair agreement will have to conform broadly to parameters that are well known and widely agreed. These will be close to the Clinton parameters: withdrawal from the Occupied Territories; dismantlement of most settlements with territorial compensation for any that remain; a form of shared sovereignty over Jerusalem; effective outside security commitments against terrorism; and a limit to refugee returns to Israel proper in order to preserve the Jewish character of the Israeli state.

It would be difficult but not impossible for Americans and Europeans to formulate an agreed statement of such parameters. Announcing this common view could give the peace process a perspective and a sense of reality that it has so far lacked. Uncertainty about the destination of any process has made room for the misrepresentations and fears that the adversaries of peace on both sides have projected onto their publics. Dissipating the bulk of this fog of fear is a prerequisite of successful resumption of the peace process.

A peace settlement will require some grim compromises on both sides; yet in addition to conveying what the settlement would entail, the Europeans and Americans can do more to communicate a vision of what a real peace would bring. Steven Simon directed in 2005 a RAND Corporation study on the infrastructure requirements of a Palestinian state. In collaboration with architect Doug Suisman, Simon developed a project that imagined the 'arc' of a Palestinian state, with Gaza and the West Bank connected by a high-speed light railway sweeping along the high ridge that forms the natural backbone of the West Bank.[22] As far as this vision might be from the daily humiliations of present-day Palestine, Simon reported to the steering group that it literally brought tears to the eyes of his Palestinian and Israeli interlocutors. However, such dreams are little more than cruel jokes if the current trajectory of immense damage to Palestinian society is not corrected. Emergency aid is not enough; there needs to be a coherent work programme with much higher levels of funding to keep public health, education and other vital services afloat, so that dysfunctional politics do not destroy Palestinian society beyond the point where a functioning state – much less visions of a modern arc – would be conceivable.

Currently the biggest impediments to a two-state solution are Israeli settlements, the security barrier where it deviates from the Green Line, and Palestinian terrorism. On the first two, America's unique influence in Israel will be critical. Neither Washington nor Jerusalem can reasonably ignore the consequences of Israeli settlements on occupied territory. American pressure would help a determined Israeli government to face down the generally unpopular but politically powerful settler lobbies.

There should be no illusions that different behaviour from Israel or the Quartet will magically render Hamas more conciliatory. Whatever truces or ambiguous offers of coexistence may have been offered, the evidence is that Hamas remains fundamentally opposed to Israel's existence. This is among the reasons that resurrection of a full-blown peace process is not, at this point, realistic. Yet, eventually, the credible interlocutor for peace will be one that has established its credentials with the Palestinian people by standing up to Israel. The Americans, Europeans and Israelis are deluded to believe that they can choose that credible Palestinian leadership. If, moreover, one believes that an eventual two-state solution is the only alternative to endless conflict – and it is truly hard to imagine another alternative – then it has to be a first principle to do no harm to the long-term viability of that solution. Collective punishment of the Palestinian people – and the current version of collective punishment of Gaza Palestinians – clearly violates that principle.

Likewise, terrorism cannot be ignored, but neither should it be used as an excuse for a kind of paralysing fatalism. In the short to medium term, the Quartet clearly has no choice but to insist on Hamas' renewing and observing its ceasefire. In the long term, the security requirements of any final-status agreement will be daunting. Even with the best of will on both sides there will almost certainly be extremist spoilers aiming to shatter peace by killing civilians.

It is hard to imagine a NATO or EU peace force interjecting itself into this situation – but it was also difficult to imagine French, German and Italian soldiers interposing themselves between Israel and Lebanon's Hizbullah until they went there in summer 2006 as part of a UN peacekeeping force.

The UNIFIL 2 mission has been hugely important and, so far, relatively successful. Its provisional success has at least partly vindicated the argument of those who argued that it was dangerous to endorse the summer 2007 conflict between Israel and Hizbullah as part of an all-fronts war against Islamist extremism. To encourage Israel in an extended war in Lebanon, seeing it as part of a proxy war between Washington and Tehran, was to neglect the narrative impact of the televised bombing of Muslim civilians. Israeli, American and European interests could only be bridged on the basis of a ceasefire and the mobilising of support for the formation of an international peacekeeping force. It was, in other words, a task of conflict resolution rather than 'victory' over terrorism.

The looming problems are, however, the fact that political authority in Lebanon is dangerously fractured, and that UNIFIL has not been able to prevent the flow of heavy weapons from Syria to Hizbullah. Both of these situations require transatlantic coordination and diplomacy. Europeans in particular need to take the lead in pressuring Damascus to cut off the flow of weapons; otherwise UNIFIL 2 is going to find itself in 2008 caught in a renewed war.

Afghanistan and Pakistan

The United States and its allies confront the real possibility of losing two wars almost simultaneously. The United States is now facing the unpleasant task, as discussed above, of radically redefining the parameters of victory and defeat in Iraq. If a new Taliban regime regains power in much or all of Afghanistan, then the half-decade of strategic response to the events of 11 September will have to be judged harshly.

If this does happen, Americans and Europeans will have ample grounds for blaming each other. Europeans can rightly say that the diversion of a war in Iraq was a devastating blow to alliance solidarity and to the concentration of sufficient resources and attention in the Afghanistan mission. Americans can justifiably complain about the flaws in strategic culture and the limited commitment, not to mention capabilities, which have hampered the effectiveness of European deployments in Afghanistan. Solidarity within Europe is also threatened: the UK has taken the lead in the expansion of NATO's International Security Assistance Force (ISAF) to six southern provinces, and is looking over its shoulder to see what kind of support it might receive from European partners.

NATO allies should remember and remind their publics of one critical point: the Afghanistan mission flows from the Article 5 declaration that they adopted on 12 September 2001, the only time that the alliance has ever invoked its central commitment to mutual defence. It will not do to repeat, however justifiably, that the US, determined to define its own war, never really took up the European allies' offer of substantial troop contributions, or that invading Iraq was counter-strategic to fighting the foes who were actually responsible for the terrorist attacks. All of this is true enough, but does not relieve either Europeans or Americans of the task at hand – following up the just and necessary destruction of the Taliban regime with a concerted commitment to stabilising and preserving Afghanistan from the kind of state failure that would once again make it a sanctuary for terrorism. It would be overly dramatic to argue that NATO's survival depends on success in Afghanistan – the alliance's institutional staying power is considerable. It is reasonable to worry, however, that if a decade of measured success – the 1990s in the Balkans – were to be followed by a decade of clear failure in Afghanistan, then the formal organisations and mechanisms of transatlantic alliance would wither, victims of their own incapacity and their leading members' lack of interest.

Strong international and allied support for a palpably justified war in Afghanistan may have obscured the immense difficulty of the undertaking. Afghanistan is larger and more populous than Iraq. Great expanses of it are ungoverned and may be ungovernable. It has suffered nearly three decades of superpower intervention and brutal civil war, culminating in a medieval reign of terror by the Taliban theocracy. Nearly half its economy depends on opium poppy.[23]

ISAF and the separately commanded *Operation Enduring Freedom* comprise, as of November 2006, roughly 40,000 troops – a modest net increase from some 31,000 in early 2006, but still not enough to overawe the resurgent Taliban, Hezb-i-Islami and foreign jihadists who are terrorising the south and east of the country. The same boots-on-the-ground to population ratio as is needed for Iraq is needed in Afghanistan; indeed, the failure to even approach an adequate ratio is much greater in Afghanistan – though the shortfall has not had, so far, quite such dramatic consequences.[24] 30,000 Afghan National Army troops – planned to eventually increase to 70,000 – have acquitted themselves well in aiding ISAF. But they bring their own problems, comprised as they are mainly of former Northern Alliance elements that are unwelcome in the Pashtun south.

Operation Enduring Freedom forces have been fighting a continuing real war in the south. ISAF, particularly in the north and the west, has addressed the critical 'hearts and minds' aspect of counter-terrorism in innovative and often effective fashion, with provincial reconstruction teams; mixed units that include civil affairs, special operations, psychological operations, and civilian experts to train army and police, strengthen legal systems, build clinics, schools and other infrastructure. But the numbers are inadequate, and there is no realistic expectation of a major increase.

What can be expected – and what might, just, be sufficient to establish a rough version of security in the country – is a combination of modest troop increases with a more effective war-fighting effort from all of the major national contingents. There are fundamental, but fixable, flaws in the way NATO organises itself for such missions. The Afghanistan mission is plagued by force-generation failures, equipment shortages and national 'caveats' – that is to say, restrictions placed by national governments on the command and deployment and the rules of engagement of their troops. Much frustration has been focused on Germany, which makes one of the largest troop contributions but which also places some of the most cumbersome restrictions on how those troops can be used. There are understandable constitutional restraints on German operations, and Germany has come a long way since the end of the Cold War in its willingness to deploy forces outside the original 'NATO area' and to use them. This is good progress, but it is perhaps not adequate to the current challenge.

NATO's problems in Afghanistan are compounded immeasurably by the fact that Taliban insurgents have sanctuary in the lawless border regions of Pakistan. Indeed, as Afghanistan expert Barnett Rubin argues, the Taliban and al-Qaeda were never decisively defeated 'but rather pushed into [Pakistan's] tribal belt'. Partly as a consequence of this, 'the main centre of terrorism "of global reach" is Pakistan'.[25] There is considerable evidence that Pakistan's intelligence service, the ISI, or at least some elements of it, is still supporting the Taliban, which it helped create in the first place.

Thus NATO finds itself, in its first ever major deployment outside Europe, to be, in effect, the regional antagonist of an American ally. It is a painful situation, for, as Rubin writes, 'few insurgencies with safe havens abroad have ever been defeated'.[26] Some call for the US and NATO to take an ever tougher line with the Musharraf government, to the point of threatening to end the relationship.[27] This is much easier said than done. To begin with, Pakistani armed forces have in fact suffered many deaths in combat against al-Qaeda, even if they tend lay off the Taliban. More to the point, it is in no Western power's interest to pressure Pakistan to the point of precipitating a civil war. The fear of a nuclear arsenal falling into the hands of Islamists may be exaggerated, but it still weighs heavily. More immediately, Pakistan feeds a serious Islamist terrorist threat in Britain in which extremist elements of the large Pakistani minority in the UK are involved. These elements travel frequently to and from Pakistan: the one successful and many attempted bombings inside Britain have been inspired or directed from Pakistani territory. Britain cannot cut itself off from this threat, and it cannot therefore afford the consequences of a civil war in Pakistan.

This complicated balance of British interests and motives in Pakistan and Afghanistan is but one example of the dilemmas and competing interests that NATO as a whole must manage without fully resolving. There is a tension between counter-insurgency and counter-narcotics; an alternation of commanders that brings an alternation between deal-making versus hardline approaches to local warlords; and the simple fact that 26 nations will not have a unified approach to fighting the Taliban and stabilising the country. Moreover, there is a danger that increased presence of foreign troops and large-scale operations in the south, especially when combined with the eradication of poppy crops, will further alienate segments of the Pashtun community there. It is unclear whether there are very useful allied discussions on these issues; NATO may need more effective consultative mechanisms to create a shared strategy among allies. The definition of what constitutes 'success' may, therefore, have to be constrained.

North Korea

The Six-Party Talks aimed at solving the North Korean nuclear crisis involve key Asia-Pacific powers, including the US and Russia. The transatlantic dimension is peripheral, although the Europeans, and especially the Security Council permanent members France and Britain, are keenly concerned about the threat to non-proliferation. North Korea poses, potentially, a frightening nexus between state failure, terrorism and nuclear weapons. The spectre of state failure is, of course, only hypothetical, since today it is probably the most tightly controlled, totalitarian state in the world. In the terms laid out by political analyst Ian Bremmer, however, it is easy to imagine it moving along a 'J-curve' from harsh dictatorial control to utter chaos, long before climbing – if it ever climbs – up the right side of the curve to democratic stability and economic growth. Indeed, rampant corruption in the country may be an early harbinger of such movement. The rulers' dependence on nearly complete isolation to maintain their control compounds the economic fragility. And it heightens concerns about the security of North Korea's nuclear materials. As Bremmer writes: 'North Korea is the world's most dangerous country because it will always be tempted to sell the world's most dangerous weapons to the world's most dangerous people.'[28] Meanwhile, the security and humanitarian implications of potential chaos have inhibited China, in particular, from exercising its economic leverage to counter the nuclear programme. This is not just an alibi, but a real concern.

The DPRK is a small, isolated country ... yet [it] is geopolitically important because it is a heavily militarised police state with a million soldiers, several million malnourished citizens, and an arsenal of the world's most dangerous weapons ... [it] is also important because it maintains a ballistic-missile capability that threatens South Korea and Japan ... It's a country close to the brink of economic ruin and large-scale starvation, which threatens to send refugees by the millions into neighbouring countries, particularly China. This flow of refugees could, in turn, produce severe food shortages in neighbouring states, breed communicable disease, provokes environmental crises, and create chaos in global financial markets. In other words, North Korea is important because of the wide range of threats it poses for the international community. Its instability is everybody's business.[29]

Triage

This list of dangerous places is a catalogue of current or foreseeable connections among terrorism, proliferation and state failure. (Each of the six countries combines at least two of the three.) The list is not nearly an infallible guide to future crises and future threats: if the years of experience since the Cold War demonstrate anything, it is that these will arise from unpredicted and perhaps unpredictable sources. The list does not include Indonesia and the rest of Southeast Asia, where an Islamist revival is taking place among the world's largest population of Muslims and in a context of struggling democracy and fractured governance. It does not include the Horn of Africa or adjacent parts of East Africa, where al-Qaeda launched the first dramatic attacks against American targets, and where continued chaos and misery presents further opportunities to terrorist groups. And it does not include a number of other African scenes of horror, such as the DRC, where civil war and state breakdown have killed nearly four million people since 1998 – the highest toll anywhere since the Second World War.

Facing all of these challenges, and others that are morally if not always strategically compelling, the US and European powers are overstretched and, because of failure in Iraq, demoralised. With NATO struggling to cope with Afghanistan, it is probably unrealistic to envisage a major, NATO-led intervention in Darfur. So the transatlantic partners need to think about the problem of triage. Where might intervention help, where will the transatlantic allies have the political interests and material capabilities to intervene effectively, how will their labours best be divided, and what international framework is there to cope with civil conflict in the absence of American or European commitment? There is no formulaic answer to any of these questions. However, the experience of the last two decades suggests three broad principles to be followed.

Firstly, transatlantic allies should effectively support the United Nations as state-builder and peacekeeper 'of first resort'.[30] This formulation comes from James Dobbins, who has vast experience with nation-building efforts in the Balkans and Afghanistan, and who over the course of several years has led teams at the RAND Corporation examining virtually all players and aspects of the problem. Dobbins makes a crucial point about the relative strengths and weakness of UN versus American and European efforts (and, implicitly, about the anti-UN dogma in the United States). During the 1990s, UN peacekeeping efforts were discredited by dramatic failures in Somalia, Rwanda and Yugoslavia. By the time of the Iraq invasion, US credibility was correspondingly high because of a sense that it had 'rescued' failed UN missions in Yugoslavia, and so easily toppled the Taliban in Afghanistan.

This history has elements of truth, but is mainly distorted. In Somalia the mission failed when the US cut its presence and expanded the mandate. In Bosnia, while it is true that the UN Secretariat's 'culture of impartiality' clouded the moral judgement of crimes approaching genocide, it was mainly a problem of the Security Council handing down 'unenforceable and crucially ambiguous mandates', and then failing to provide the forces to enforce them.[31] The United States played its part in this failure. But the more important point is that the UN embarked upon a lengthy process of lessons learned. This could be seen most dramatically in the UN's report on its performance in Srebrenica, a report that was commissioned and endorsed by Secretary-General Kofi Annan, and which was scathing about the UN Secretariat's own failings:

> The Secretariat had convinced itself early on that the broader use of force by the international community was beyond our mandate and anyway undesirable … The cardinal lesson of Srebrenica is that a deliberate and systematic attempt to terrorise, expel or murder an entire people must be met decisively with all necessary means. In the Balkans, in this decade, this lesson has had to be learned not once, but twice.[32]

In contrast to this soul-searching, the United States has in recent times engaged in a policy of deliberate amnesia. This is one reason why, as Dobbins has documented with one of his RAND teams, UN operations taken together in fact show a better success rate than do US operations.[33]

> The United Nations has done a better job of learning from its mistakes than has the United States over the past 15 years ... Throughout the 1990s, the United States got steadily better at nation-building. The Haitian operation was better managed than Somalia, Bosnia better than Haiti, and Kosovo better than Bosnia. The US learning curve has not been sustained into the current decade. The Bush administration that took office in 2001 initially disdained nation-building as an unsuitable activity for US forces. When compelled to engage in such missions, first in Afghanistan and then Iraq, the administration sought to break with the strategies and institutional responses that had been honed throughout the 1990s to deal with these challenges ... The United States tends to staff each new operation as if it were its first, and is destined to be the last.[34]

It is clearly probable that the relative UN success also has to do with the fact that blue-helmet operations are in many cases less demanding than those upon which the United States and its allies have embarked. But this points, conversely, to a UN strength – minimally equipped, less highly trained UN troops are cheaper and easier to deploy, compared to Western forces.

The model for many of the more intractable cases will be some combination of limited Western forces and more numerous UN peacekeepers. There is a recent, somewhat astonishing example of how successful this can be in the experience since 2002 of the DRC, where a series of limited EU deployments has provided support at key junctures to a revitalised UN peacekeeping operation. The combination has helped turn around – at least for the moment – one of the most catastrophically failed states in the world.[35] For the UN, such so-called 'punctuated' EU deployments have had the effect not only of bringing to bear more capable EU forces in specific crises; they have also impressed local combatants with the possibility that that the UN has major European powers behind it. For the EU, it is easier politically to get member states to sign up for time-limited deployments with a plan to hand over to UN peacekeepers.

Americans and Europeans should also be more ready to contribute troops directly to UN peacekeeping operations. The deployment of European troops to the Lebanon operation – UNIFIL 2 – in 2006 is a welcome step in this regard. Over the ten years prior to this, the Europeans and the Americans neglected UN peacekeeping operations, and left global peacekeeping to woefully ill-equipped local forces. They were also careful to insulate their own interventions (in Sierra Leone, Côte d'Ivoire, the DRC) from UN operations. Such separation is politically unwelcome, as it damages the sense of equality and the universal character of the UN. The aim should be to restore, or create, a level of effectiveness and confidence in UN operations that will allow Western contingents to participate fully, as they did in the late 1980s and the first half of the 1990s.

Secondly, the transatlantic partners need to build up capacity and knowledge for vital peacekeeping and stabilisation missions. European military staffs do appreciate that such missions are their future; yet, nearly two decades after the end of the Cold War, too many of their forces are still configured for territorial defence on the European central front. The American military undertook considerable soul-searching and rethinking after its initial, and fateful, failure to establish real security in immediate post-invasion Iraq. Having decided in effect to forget about counter-insurgency operations after the trauma of Vietnam, US military colleges and planning staffs are now taking the opposite view, recognising that, however Iraq turns out, it will not be the last such mission.

Thirdly, NATO and the EU need to better manage, if they cannot completely end, their rivalry, and not let it become a cause for inaction. Americans need to better understand and accept the aspirations for an autonomous European defence capability. Europeans should be attentive to the problem of duplication, even if some duplication is unavoidable, and they should also be willing to recognise the cases where NATO's greater capabilities are required. Beyond these two somewhat obvious stipulations, there is no clear formula for deciding whether an operation should be under NATO or EU command. But there are some principles that can be discerned from examining the roles that NATO has recently played and the other, so far more limited cases, where European troops have deployed under EU command, and considering the future scenarios to which EU missions could be most appropriate.

In practice, NATO's energies are now increasingly being redirected towards three kinds of operation:

- The ad hoc commitment of stabilisation forces in support of American-led operations (e.g. NATO's support for ISAF in

Afghanistan, leading in 2003 to NATO assuming full command of and responsibility for the operation).

- Naval control operations in support of counter-terrorism or counter-proliferation (*Operation Active Endeavor* in the Mediterranean, the European contribution to naval control operations in the Indian Ocean following 11 September).
- The provision of doctrine, training and interoperability so that the Europeans (at least some of them) and the Americans can work together across the spectrum of military operations (the creation of Allied Command Transformation and the NATO Response Force in 2002).

Afghanistan has clearly settled NATO's 'out of area' debate – there is no 'NATO area' anymore. But this does not tell us anything about where NATO's priorities should be, substantively or geographically. From a substantive standpoint, ought the alliance to be open-ended, and ready to assume any kind of task, or should it be selective, and at least give priority to some sets of issues over others? It is in the nature of the alliance as it now is not to offer definite answers to these questions. Nevertheless, some preferences must be developed, and at least broad criteria identified for which kinds of issue NATO is and is not suited to address. Three possible guidelines come to mind:

- The alliance should make it a priority to act on problems that represent a common challenge to the security of Europe and the United States. Essential to the identity of an alliance is the notion of common threats, and common security objectives. An alliance that increasingly rested on undertaking humanitarian or disaster relief operations would lose its identity in the end.
- The alliance should act on issues on which there is genuine agreement among the allies, where it is likely to be able to play a significant role, and where there is a prospect of NATO's deliberations influencing the overall strategy of the common action. Afghanistan meets these requirements.
- By contrast, it should avoid playing visibly ancillary roles, or allowing its involvement to be used to present a false appearance of unity of purpose where there is very little, or none, as in Iraq.

As for the geographical scope of NATO's activities, again it is more a matter of using sound political judgement in specific contexts than of imposing a priori limitations. Clearly, the alliance could make a contribution to naval operations anywhere. (European navies have contributed to exercises in the Far East under the Proliferation Security Initiative, which, although not a NATO initiative, has a strong transatlantic dimension.)

As regards ground operations, Europeans and Americans have already acted together in very distant places. But NATO as such should probably avoid intervening in places where there is a regional organisation better suited to carrying out the task (in Haiti in 2004, although US and French forces were the first involved, at no point was a resort to NATO envisaged, the Organisation of American States and the UN being the natural frameworks for an operation in the region).

Similarly, there is a genuine question mark over whether NATO will find a role for itself in sub-Saharan Africa, whereas the Europeans appear eager and able to intervene. This readiness to act should be welcomed by NATO, and the organisation's discontent on seeing the EU act in the DRC in support of the UN, and the appearance of competition between the EU and NATO in Darfur, have been deplorable; such rivalry needs to be avoided.

Notwithstanding the reluctance of major powers to intervene in Darfur, more help there is feasible. Following their first meeting as leaders of their respective countries in July 2007, French President Nicolas Sarkozy and British Prime Minister Gordon Brown announced that Britain and France would co-sponsor a UN resolution calling for an immediate ceasefire and a hybrid UN–African Union peacekeeping force to be dispatched to Darfur. They also stated their intention to travel jointly to the region once the resolution had been passed by the Security Council. At around the same time, EU nations began planning under the European Security and Defence Policy for an interim mission of some 3,000 European troops, backed by a UN police force, which would protect the camps in eastern Chad containing refugees from Darfur and internally displaced persons. This is important not least because militias responsible for atrocities in Darfur are using eastern Chad as a rear base.

The EU formally endorsed the initiative, actively supported by the new French Foreign Minister Bernard Kouchner, in late July. The plan also received swift expression of support from US Secretary of State Rice, with the implication that theological disputes about NATO vs the EU might become a thing of the past.

The earlier success of EU involvement in the DRC has contributed to a rethinking of the EU's plans for its own autonomous military capability. Behind its original headline goal of December 1999 – to be able to deploy up to 60,000 troops overseas within 60 days for at least a year[36] – there were at least some European strategists who hoped that the EU would be able to conduct the equivalent of the Kosovo War on its own. It has not attained anything like this capability – although it should be added that EU states currently do have this number of troops deployed far beyond the EU's borders, some of them in quite demanding operations.[37] But more recently, with leadership from Britain and France, the EU has turned its focus to standing up 'battlegroups' – spearhead forces numbering some 1,500 soldiers that are able to move quickly to stabilise a crisis, pending replacement by larger UN units.

The art of the possible

At the turn of this century there came a high tide of optimism, in some quarters at least, about the Atlantic alliance's capability and collective will to act, in effect, as a state-building consortium that could rescue some of the most vulnerable segments of humanity from genocidal conflict and humanitarian distress. This optimism was expressed in two speeches by Prime Minister Tony Blair: the first in April 1999 in Chicago, in which he laid out a 'doctrine of international community' that outlined the principles on which NATO could be said to be acting in its air war over Kosovo; the second at the Labour Party Conference in October 2001, in which he plausibly linked the 'scar on the conscience of the world' of state failure and misery in Africa to the anarchic conditions that had enabled al-Qaeda.[38]

This optimism has now receded dramatically. Four years after the American-led invasion to change its regime, Iraq itself is taking on the attributes of a failed state. This result could have unsettling consequences for other efforts to take on state-building responsibilities, as was recognised just weeks after the invasion by former US diplomat Morton Abramowitz:

> Bush has probably achieved, inadvertently, what he campaigned for: getting the United States out of nation-building … He has done this by embarking on nation-building unprecedented since World War II and in a land that we do not know well and that does not play to our strengths. And it was done, it is now clear, with little effective planning and with largely unexamined notions of what can be accomplished.[39]

A certain retrenchment is probably inevitable. The wealthy European and North American democracies should not imagine, however, that they can simply get out of the game. For all the recent trauma and discord around the issue of intervention, working to meet the challenge of failed states is in fact one of the clearest examples of fairly recent transatlantic cooperation. In the Balkans, at least, that cooperation must be judged as a modest success. On a smaller scale, Britain and France have managed with very limited military deployments to bring some improvement to Sierra Leone and Côte d'Ivoire. European (mainly French) troops under EU auspices have brought some relief to Bunia in the DRC. And while the ultimate success of the Afghanistan operation is far from assured, it is worth bearing in mind that both the war and the post-war stabilisation operation have been more or less uncontroversial in transatlantic terms. Indeed, the post-war mission in Afghanistan, for all of its current troubles, may provide the best model for what NATO as an institution can and should do with itself. If 'nation-building is the inescapable responsibility of the world's only superpower', as James Dobbins insists,[40] it is a responsibility that the United States is utterly unable – for material, political and cultural reasons – to shoulder alone. It is, therefore, also an inescapable subject for transatlantic cooperation.

But the consensus for continuing that cooperation will have to be built around a more modest definition of its aims. An aggressive strategy of democratisation through the use or threat of military force is too divisive and will not succeed. It is divisive because there is a genuine underlying disagreement between European conservatism and American ambition. It will not work not least because the chaos created by the botched regime change in Iraq has largely discredited the idea of American-championed democracy, throughout the Middle East at least.

The failure in Iraq has implications that go beyond the competence in execution of a particular American policy. The successful or at least semi-successful interventions in the Balkans involved countries in which state control had already broken down. Since the Second World War, cases of military force successfully being used to destroy an intact regime and rebuild order on top of it have been rare, if there have in fact been any. One might cite the cases of Germany and Japan, but both these countries had reservoirs of certain kinds of experience on which to draw, including, fleetingly, democratic experience. In their institutions, culture and levels of popular education, they had the software of advanced, effective states, and that software was preserved rather than eradicated by the occupying forces. This is a crucial point, as political scientist Shibley Telhami argues persuasively that:

> once the institutions of sovereignty are destroyed in any state, especially one with a heterogeneous society, the odds are against

any effort to build a stable alternative in the same generation. In the absence of effective central authority, all it takes is a small, determined minority to prevent unity.[41]

It was a quarter-century ago that suicide terrorism drove American and French forces out of Lebanon, a precedent that US and other Coalition leaders might have pondered when they imagined that their troops would be welcomed into an easily pacified Iraq. There are times when it is necessary, strategically or morally, to intervene with military force, but caution is always in order. Forces that intervene for the best of motives against the most atrocious humanitarian outrages can find that they outstay their welcome. As a general rule, moreover, it is safe to assume that the more ambitious the attempt to reorder a society, the more resistance is likely to be aroused. For this reason, America and Europe will find it easier to come together around basic principles of humanitarian stabilisation and the defence of human rights than around radical democratisation. In any event, they should know what they are getting into.

Ambitions and Limits of a Transatlantic Partnership

The idea that everything changed on 11 September 2001 has brought more confusion than clarity to transatlantic relations. It is understandable, given the shock and horror of that day, and it does reflect aspects of the transformation in the nature of what threatens both the West and the wider world. The threat of major inter-state war has receded, if not vanished, while another class of threats at the intersection of globalisation and chaos has become more important. These threats include nuclear proliferation, state failure, transnational terrorism, pandemic disease and environmental catastrophe.

But that the ranking of threats has changed does not mean that the basic interests or purposes of American and European allies are unrecognisable. In order to understand what the alliance should be dedicated to in the future, it is helpful to remember what it has achieved in the recent past.

In the immediate post-Cold War years, the United States and Europe were satisfied powers, in a world enjoying an unprecedented degree of security, with no violent conflict among major players in sight. As a consequence, they adopted an essentially conservative strategic agenda dedicated to preserving the status quo: the territorial status quo, globally as well as in Europe; and the nuclear status quo. The pursuit of this agenda in the decade after 1989 brought some notable achievements:

- the peaceful reunification of Germany and the more or less amicable dissolution of the Warsaw Pact;

- the 1991 Gulf War, which sustained the territorial status quo while anticipating a 'new world order'[1] that had recognisable roots in the old one;
- a successful management of the Soviet Union's territorial break-up and nuclear succession;
- a conservative solution to the break-up of Yugoslavia, with partition carried out along its former internal borders, the contagion of territorial claims avoided elsewhere in Europe, and mass ethnic cleansing opposed, albeit belatedly, with NATO military force;
- indefinite extension of the NPT, which further consolidated the nuclear status quo.

This was a modest and realistic vision, well suited to the interests of the West, and on the whole, a considerable success. It implicitly supported giving former adversaries such as Russia, emerging powers such as China, and other players including, notably, the Arab world, a real stake in the global order. Its defence depended mainly on the United States and on a transatlantic partnership in which post-Maastricht Europe would play a more active role.

But the vision had limitations. It satisfied neither American idealism nor European ambitions. For Americans it is always likely to be a problem that defence of the status quo is uninspiring and, at times, constraining. Europe, for its part, did not transform itself into a truly global partner. Individual European states did make progress in adapting their militaries to new, expeditionary operations, and they significantly relaxed their inhibitions about using force abroad. The EU also contributed significantly through its own enlargement to expanding stability in Europe. Enlargement, however, though a resounding success in its own terms, was achieved at the expense of the EU's internal cohesion, the robustness of its political identity and the level of public support for integration.

The conservative vision was also limited in its capacity to address the emerging security challenges that manifested themselves at the sub-state and transnational levels. New concepts that did seek to address them, such as humanitarian intervention, were in tension with the status quo, and therefore the conservative vision, insofar as this conservatism implied a greater regard for the principles of non-use of force and the consolidation of territorial sovereignty.

These underlying sources of transatlantic difficulties predate 11 September and the invasion of Iraq. It is worth re-emphasising that, since those events, Europe and the United States have focused on a remarkably congruent list of threats: terrorism, proliferation and reckless or failed states, and, increasingly on both sides, climate change. It is, however, the potential systematic convergence of the first three threats – creating, for example, a continuing nightmare of WMD terrorism associated with accomplice rogue states – that is likely to continue to preoccupy US policymakers even after the Bush administration leaves office. For Europeans, terrorism and proliferation remain largely separate issues, on the whole to be combated separately, and undeterrable rogue states are not high on their list of concerns.

More broadly, some Americans concluded after 11 September that the status quo was no longer tenable, and that the United States should now regard itself as a revolutionary power – a view that found its way into US policy under the heading of the 'transformation' of the Middle East. Even without this policy's most spectacular manifestation, war in Iraq, the new American radicalism was likely to have caused further transatlantic tension. Europeans remained more sensitive to the achievements of a status quo agenda – the less frequent resort to the use of force, and the hitherto successful inhibition of the proliferation of nuclear weapons through arms control – and were not eager to embrace an agenda for revolutionary change in the Middle East or anywhere else.

There are new circumstances, of course: the United States has become much more subdued as a result of its misadventures in Iraq, and George W. Bush's departure from office in January 2009 will complete the handover to new governments in each of the key alliance capitals. Though transatlantic differences cannot be expected to disappear, nor are they irreconcilable. Europeans are not averse to promoting democracy, including in the Middle East. They were more comfortable, however, with Clinton's strategy of enlargement and engagement, of using favourable circumstances to tip the scales with occasional and opportunistic interventions (of the kind that could be seen more recently in US and French diplomacy towards Lebanon) than with a systematic campaign for radical change in the world's most volatile region.

Ultimately, the real and abiding transatlantic tension probably lies here, not in specific disagreements about Iraq, Palestine or a nuclear Iran, but in the tension between those whom Lawrence Freedman has identified as 'visionaries' and 'counter-visionaries'. The counter-visionaries – more often than not Europeans – are not reactionaries, but cautious heeders of Max Weber's warning that there needs to be an 'ethic of responsibility' as well as an 'ethic of ultimate ends'.[2] In this dichotomy, the 'fundamental philosophical issue', Freedman writes, is 'strategic. It concerns the readiness to acknowledge and adjust to the power of others, however undeserved, illegitimate, inconvenient and awkward this power may be.'[3]

The Bush administration's visionary pursuit of ultimate ends with hardly any ballast of strategic reckoning has clearly damaged the alliance as well as diminishing the strategic position of the United States. Yet, it is just as obvious that any isolationist collapse of the American vision would impoverish both sides of the Atlantic and the world at large. Freedman finds Weber's Weimar circumstances also relevant in this regard:

> [As] Weber also recognised, at certain times some vision of a better world was also essential. Only if leaders could persuade people to reach out for the impossible would they achieve the merely possible. These were times of upheaval when there was no status quo readily available to defend, so it was the task of political leadership to describe a better future without adopting strategies that were bound to make things worse.[4]

Transposed to the present, this logic would suggest that a status quo alliance is only viable insofar as it recognises and adapts when the status quo is no longer sustainable. But equally, the Atlantic alliance cannot be the revolutionary vehicle that many Americans might prefer it to be. Consensus-building is an inherently conservative undertaking, and sovereign allies can only be pushed so far.

The propositions laid out in this paper are intended to satisfy both some degree of American vision and European caution. They ambitiously aim to persuade Iran to forgo nuclear weapons, but on the conservative basis of preserving the status quo of the NPT regime. They urge the consolidation and more active enforcement of international norms against states facilitating genocide, terrorism and proliferation – but based on the simultaneous acknowledgement of certain abiding prerogatives of state sovereignty, even where the regimes in question are objectionable. Their promotion of human rights and democracy is a more or less conservative approach, grounded in the alliance experience of détente and realpolitik that proved effective in the long and patient struggle of the Cold War. The propositions regarding stability in Iraq and state-building in Palestine acknowledge that success requires help from entrenched and mainly undemocratic regimes in the Middle East. They propose state-building roles for NATO and EU forces on the basis of lessons learned over the past 20 years, and the continuing importance of traditional UN peacekeeping. Even the paper's most radical hope, for the creation of new instruments of global governance to combat climate change, is expressed on the assumption that humankind will be moved by the deeply conservative impulse to preserve its planetary inheritance.

The compromises inherent in these proposals present a burden and a choice, primarily to the United States, for the simple reason that only the United States has the power and autonomy such that it can still try to go it alone. There will no doubt be occasions when it does act alone, unwilling to accept allied restraints. In each case, however, it should be careful to consider whether unilateralism really is in the American interest.[5]

On all sides, the transatlantic partners will need to temper their expectations of one another over the coming years. Europeans cannot expect America to commit itself always and forever to formal multilateral restraint. Americans should not expect Europeans to embark on ambitious schemes of international reorder. The pursuit of grand new architectures is at best a distraction, at worst likely to mire the alliance in unnecessary philosophical disputes. Circumstances on the ground – and the inevitable adjustment to reality that they will require, as in Iraq – will be much more important. Attitudes will matter more than doctrines. A good start for the United States would be more strategy and less ideology; for Europe, less reliance on order and principles, and more readiness for action.

APPENDIX

IISS Transatlantic Steering Group and Workshop Participants

This Adelphi Paper grew out of a two-year series of meetings in London, Geneva, Washington, Paris and Rome convening key transatlantic figures in a regular steering group together with other invited experts. The authors gratefully acknowledge the participants' input and advice. However the views expressed in this paper, and any errors, are the authors' alone. Professional identifications correspond to the time of the project meetings.

Graham Allison	John F. Kennedy School of Government, Harvard University
Lucia Annunziata	*La Stampa*
Erica Barks-Ruggles	US Department of State
Nomi Bar-Yaacov	Foreign Policy Adviser on Middle Eastern Affairs
Avis Bohlen	Former US Assistant Secretary of State for Arms Control
Martin Briens	Political–Military Counsellor, Embassy of France to the United States
David Calleo	School of Advanced International Studies, Johns Hopkins University
Christopher Chyba	Stanford University
Richard Caplan	University of Oxford
Chester Crocker	Georgetown University; former US Assistant Secretary of State for African Affairs

Marta Dassu	Aspen Institute Italia
James Dobbins	RAND Corporation; former US Assistant Secretary of State for Europe
Toby Dodge	International Institute for Strategic Studies
Robert Einhorn	Center for Strategic and International Studies
Richard Falkenrath	Brookings Institute; former US Deputy Homeland Security Advisor
Mark Fitzpatrick	International Institute for Strategic Studies
Simon Fraser	Director for Strategy and Innovation, UK Foreign and Commonwealth Office
Sir Lawrence Freedman	King's College London
Bastian Giegerich	International Institute for Strategic Studies
Dennis Gormley	Monterey Institute
Charles Grant	Centre for European Reform
Rita Hauser	President, The Hauser Foundation
François Heisbourg	Chairman, International Institute for Strategic Studies
Tim Huxley	International Institute for Strategic Studies
Tom Inglesby	Center for Biosecurity, University of Pittsburgh
Susan Koch	Senior Advisor to the US Under Secretary of State for Arms Control and International Security
Heinrich Kreft	Deputy Director of Policy Planning, German Foreign Ministry
Charles Kupchan	Council on Foreign Relations
Ellen Laipson	The Henry L. Stimson Center; former Vice Chairman of the US National Intelligence Council
Pierre Lévy	Policy Planning Director, French Ministry of Foreign Affairs
Gustav Lindstrom	European Union Institute for Security Studies
David Makovsky	Washington Institute for Near East Policy
Michael McClay	Hakluyt and Company; former political adviser to Douglas Hurd and Carl Bildt
Roberto Menotti	Aspen Institute Italia
Michael Moodie	Former Director of the Chemical and Biological Arms Control Institute
General Klaus Naumann	Former Chairman of the Military Committee, NATO
Jonathan Paris	University of Oxford
Dame Pauline Neville-Jones	Qinetiq; former Chairman of UK Joint Intelligence Committee
Anne Pringle	Director of Policy Planning, UK Foreign and Commonwealth Office

Mitchell Reiss	Special Envoy to the Northern Ireland Peace Process; former Director for Policy Planning, US Department of State
Sir Adam Roberts	University of Oxford
Lord (George) Robertson	Former Secretary-General, NATO, and former UK Defence Secretary
Fidel Sendagorta	Director of Policy Planning, Spanish Ministry of Foreign Affairs
Gary Schmitt	Project for the New American Century
Kori Shake	US National Security Council
Steven N. Simon	RAND Corporation; former Senior Director for Transnational Threats, US National Security Council
Walter Slocombe	Caplin & Drysdale; former US Under Secretary of Defense for Policy
Volker Stanzel	Political Director, German Foreign Ministry
Jonathan Stevenson	International Institute for Strategic Studies
Sir Hilary Synnott	International Institute for Strategic Studies
Terence Taylor	International Institute for Strategic Studies
Ashley Tellis	Carnegie Endowment for International Peace; former Senior Director, US National Security Council
Bruno Tertrais	Fondation pour la récherche stratégique
Lord (William) Wallace	London School of Economics
Matthew Waxman	Principal Deputy Director, Policy Planning Staff, US Department of State
Lord (George) Weidenfeld	Founder and Chairman, Weidenfeld and Nicolson

The meetings were made possible through generous support from the Carnegie Corporation of New York, the Robert Bosch Foundation and the Ford Foundation.

NOTES

Introduction

1   On the Jacksonian tradition in US foreign
    policy, see Walter Russell Mead, *Special
    Providence: American Foreign Policy and
    How It Changed the World* (New York:
    Knopf, 2001).

2   The Stern Review recently estimated
    that the cost of substantially reducing
    the impact of climate change would be
    1% of global GDP each year to 2050. See
    Nicholas Stern, *The Economics of Climate
    Change: The Stern Review* (Cambridge:

Cambridge University Press, 2006), pp.
xv–xix, http://www.hm-treasury.gov.
uk/independent_reviews/stern_review_
economics_climate_change/stern_
review_report.cfm.

3   Gregg Easterbrook, 'Case Closed: The
    Debate about Global Warming Is Over',
    Issues in Governance Studies, no. 3, Brookings
    Institution, June 2006, pp. 1, 6–8.

4   We are indebted to Jeffrey Mazo for sug-
    gesting this comparison.

Chapter One

1   The current consensus between Euro-
    peans and Americans that terrorism is
    the security threat of greatest concern
    predates 11 September: at the 1999 NATO
    summit in Washington, for example, ter-
    rorism alone was cited as an actual, rather
    than a potential, danger to the alliance,
    constituting 'a serious threat to peace,
    security and stability that can threaten the
    territorial integrity of States'. Washington
    Summit Communiqué, 'An Alliance for
    the 21st Century', 24 April 1999, http://
    www.nato.int/docu/pr/1999/p99-064e.
    htm. Opinion polls show a similar conver-
    gence, not only in the ranking of the threat

but also in the perception of its intensity.
In 2002, 86% of French people perceived
terrorism to be a 'very big' or 'moderately
big' problem for their country, compared
with 87% of Americans. Pew Research
Center for the People and the Press, 2002
Global Attitudes Survey, Final Topline, p.
23, http://people-press.org/reports/pdf/
165topline.pdf.

2   Independent Panel to Review Depart-
    ment of Defense Detention Operations,
    *Final Report of the Independent Panel
    to Review DoD Detention Operations*
    ('Schlesinger Report') (Arlington, VA:
    Independent Panel to Review Department

of Defense Detention Operations, August 2004), p. 16.

3 See for example a survey conducted by Populus in July 2006, which revealed that 13% of British Muslims regarded the bombers of 7/7 as 'martyrs', Alexandra Frean and Rajeev Syal, 'Muslim Britain Split Over "Martyrs" of 7/7', *The Times*, 4 July 2006, http://www.timesonline.co.uk/article/0,,22989-2254764,00.html.

4 See Stern, *The Economics of Climate Change.*

5 Michael Howard, 'What's in a Name?', *Foreign Affairs*, vol. 81, no. 1, January–February 2002, pp. 8–13. The European approach to this issue is informed by long-standing experience of the value to counter-terrorist campaigns of denying the existence of a state of war, as it has been evidenced in relation to the IRA in Northern Ireland, ETA in the Basque province of Spain, the Baader–Meinhof group in Germany and the Red Brigades in Italy. The 2006 French white paper on domestic security measures against terrorism explicitly states that 'France has decided to remain within a peacetime logic. The fact that it is using its armed forces in the fight against terrorism does not contradict this choice', and declares 'We must marginalise those who undertake terrorist acts, reminding everyone that these are not warriors, but criminals. You do not go to war against criminals', Secrétaire général de la defense nationale, *White Paper on Domestic Security Against Terrorism,* Paris, 2006, pp. 114 and 117, http://www.ambafrance-bd.org/IMG/pdf/livre_anglais.pdf.

6 The White House, *The President's State of the Union Address* (Washington DC: The White House, 29 January 2002), http://www.whitehouse.gov/news/releases/2002/01/20020129-11.html.

7 The White House, *The National Security Strategy of the United States of America* (Washington DC: The White House, September 2002), p.15, http://www.whitehouse.gov/nsc/nss.pdf.

8 The White House: *The National Security Strategy of the United States of America*

(Washington DC: The White House, 16 March 2006), http://www.whitehouse.gov/nsc/nss/2006/intro.html.

9 'I'm a war president. I make decisions here in the Oval Office on foreign policy matters with war on my mind … And the American people need to know they got a president who sees the world the way it is.' George W. Bush, *Meet the Press*, NBC, 8 February 2004, http://www.msnbc.msn.com/id/4179618/.

10 Richard Haass, 'Drop the "War on Terrorism" Metaphor', *The Daily Star* (Lebanon), 12 August 2006.

11 See 'A Strong Military for a New Century', speech delivered by John Edwards, former US senator, New York, 23 May 2007, http://www.cfr.org/publication/13432/ and 'Remarks of Senator Barack Obama to the Chicago Council on Global Affairs', speech delivered by Barack Obama, US senator, Chicago, 23 April 2007, http://www.thechicagocouncil.org/dynamic_page.php?id=64.

12 A French justice official later said that 'the government gave the FBI "everything we had" on Moussaoui'. Romesh Ratnesar and Michael Weisskopf, 'How the FBI Blew the Case', *Time*, 3 June 2002.

13 Dana Priest, 'Help From France Key in Covert Operations: Paris's "Alliance Base" Targets Terrorists', *The Washington Post*, 3 July 2005, p. A01.

14 'Regierungserklärung von Bundeskanzler Schröder zur aktuellen Lage nach Beginn der Operation gegen den internationalen Terrorismus in Afghanistan', 11 October 2001, http://archiv.bundesregierung.de/regierungserklaerung,-59425/Regierungserklaerung-von-Bunde.htm (translation by author).

15 Priest, 'Help From France Key in Covert Operations'.

16 See for example Michael Inacker, 'Deutsche Soldaten jagen Al Qaida', *Frankfurter Allgemeine Sonntagszeitung*, 24 February 2002.

17 Barry Lando, 'Terrorism Cooperation: Despite Pinpricks, France Quietly Helps

U.S.', *International Herald Tribune*, 16 May 2003.

18 Adam Roberts, 'The "War on Terror" in Historical Perspective', *Survival*, vol. 47, no. 2, Summer 2005, pp. 101–130.

19 Ministry of Defence, *The Strategic Defence Review: A New Chapter* (London: The Stationery Office, July 2002), p.10.

20 *2006 National Security Strategy of the United States of America*, pp. 9–11.

21 Six French nationals, detained at Guantanamo and then held upon their return to France, were tried in July 2006 for the crime of 'criminal conspiracy in relation to a terrorist enterprise'. The trial was disrupted by the revelation that French government agents had interviewed the detainees during their imprisonment at Guantanamo. New hearings are now scheduled for December 2007. Craig S. Smith, '6 Former Guantanamo Detainees on Trial in Paris', *New York Times*, 4 July 2006; Michel Moutot, 'French Intelligence in Spotlight in "Guantanamo six" trial', Agence France Presse, 27 September 2006.

22 Council of Europe Committee on Legal Affairs and Human Rights, *Alleged Secret Detentions and Unlawful Inter-State Transfers Involving Council of Europe Member States*, Draft Report, 7 June 2006.

23 See Olivier Roy, 'Intifada on the Housing Estates or a Young Underclass in Revolt?', http://www.diplomatie.gouv.fr/fr/IMG/pdf/0501-ROY-GB-2.pdf; originally published as 'Intifada des banlieues ou émeutes des jeunes declasses?' in *Esprit*, no. 12, December 2005.

24 See for example Spencer Ackerman, 'Religious Protection: Why American Muslims Haven't Turned to Terrorism', *The New Republic*, 12 December 2005, pp. 18–21, 28–30.

Chapter Two

1 Francis Fukuyama, 'Invasion of the Isolationists', *New York Times*, 31 August 2005, p. A19.

2 Charles Krauthammer, 'The Unipolar Moment', *Foreign Affairs*, vol. 70, no. 1, Winter 1990–91, pp. 23–33.

3 For more on the A.Q. Khan network, see the International Institute for Strategic Studies, *Nuclear Black Markets: Pakistan, A.Q. Khan and the rise of proliferation networks: A net assessment* (London: IISS, 2007).

4 Chapter Seven of the UN Charter concerns Security Council 'action with respect to threats to the peace, breaches of the peace, and acts of aggression'. Article 41 covers non-violent measures available to the Security Council, such as economic sanctions and the interruption of diplomatic relations; Article 42 covers the use of force and other military measures.

5 Marc Weller, 'The US, Iraq and the Use of Force in a Unipolar World', *Survival*, vol. 41, no. 4, Winter 1999–2000, p. 89.

6 Ron Suskind, *The One Percent Doctrine* (New York: Simon and Schuster, 2006).

7 Gareth Evans, 'When Is It Right to Fight?', *Survival*, vol. 46, no. 3, Autumn 2004, p. 65.

8 See 'La dissuasion nucléaire comme outil de prévention', speech delivered by Jacques Chirac, President of France, Brest, 19 January 2006, http://www.diplomatie.gouv.fr/actu/bulletin.asp?liste=20060120.html#Chapitre1.

9 Richard K. Betts, 'The Osirak Fallacy', *National Interest*, no. 83, Spring 2006, pp. 22–5.

10 The E3–Iran diplomacy is a good illustration of the organic development of EU foreign policy in general. It cannot be effective as a committee or consensus project of 25 (now 27) members of equal voice. So core groups – to some extent self-appointed but enjoying the tacit acquiescence of the EU membership as a whole – take the lead, acting to

some extent as proxies for the rest. This works best when the proxies occupy the EU's centre of gravity for a given problem area. Thus Germany and Poland formed a natural core group to push for a democratic resolution to Ukraine's Christmas 2004 elections crisis. Likewise, in previous 'contact groups' of leading European states pursuing Balkans peace initiatives along with the US and Russia, it eventually was deemed important to add Italy to the troika of France, Britain and Germany, because of Italy's geographical proximity to the Balkans, hosting of US airbases, and other entanglements of interest. For the EU's Iranian diplomacy, having Berlin as part of the core group along with the relatively more hawkish London and Paris was important, not only because of Germany's economic clout and relations with Iran, but also because Germans are good representatives of the 'softer' views of some other EU member states. The involvement of Javier Solana, High Representative for Common Foreign and Security Policy, which today is an integral part of the E3, reinforced this approach. One often-overlooked fact is that since June 2006 Solana has been acting as executive agent, not only for the EU as a whole in his discussions with the Iranians, but also for Russia, China and the US.

11 Iran thus unilaterally terminated the so-called Paris Agreement, reached between the E3 and Iran, which gave a comprehensive and detailed description of activities to be suspended.

12 Transatlantic Trends, *Key Findings 2006*, 6 September 2006, http://www.transatlantictrends.org/trends/doc/2006_TT_Key%20Findings%20FINAL.pdf.

13 KEDO was established in 1995 by the US, Japan and South Korea (other states later joined) to provide North Korea with heavy fuel oil and light-water reactors in return for the freezing and eventual dismantlement of its nuclear programme under the terms of the Agreed Framework. The light-water reactor project was terminated in May 2006.

14 The PSI's 'Statement of Interdiction Principles' was adopted at the Paris meeting of participants in September 2003, http://usinfo.state.gov/products/pubs/proliferation/#statement.

15 'Physical protection controls' are physical measures such as perimeter fences and guard patrols for safeguarding nuclear assets against theft and smuggling.

16 See Paula A. DeSutter, US assistant secretary for verification, compliance, and implementation, 'The New U.S. Approach to Verification', remarks to Carnegie International Nonproliferation Conference, Washington DC, 7 November 2005.

17 Christopher F. Chyba, 'Biological Terrorism and Public Health', *Survival*, no. 43, no. 1, Spring 2001, p. 99.

18 Shankar Vedantam, 'WHO Assails Wealthy Nations on Bioterror; Coordination of Defenses Poor in Simulation; U.S. Support for Agency Questioned', *Washington Post*, 5 November 2003, p. A8.

19 *EU Strategy Against the Proliferation of Weapons of Mass Destruction (WMD)*, adopted by the European Council in December 2003, see http://ec.europa.eu/external_relations/us/sum06_04/fact/wmd.pdf.

20 The 2002 G8 Global Partnership Against the Spread of Weapons and Materials of Mass Destruction committed G8 states to raising up to $20 billion over ten years for cooperation projects to address non-proliferation, disarmament, counter-terrorism and nuclear safety issues. The initiative also included a commitment to a set of six principles designed to prevent terrorists from gaining access to weapons or materials of mass destruction. See http://www.state.gov/e/rls/rm/2002/12190.htm.

21 See 'Remarks by the President on Weapons of Mass Destruction Proliferation', speech delivered by George W. Bush to the National Defense University, 11 February 2004, http://www.whitehouse.

gov/news/releases/2004/02/20040211-4.
html.

22 'Concept for a Multilateral Mechanism
for Reliable Access to Nuclear Fuel'.
Mentions can be found at http://
www.iaea.org/NewsCenter/Statements/
2006/ebsp2006n009.html and http://
www.state.gov/t/isn/rls/rm/85176.htm.

23 Pierre Goldschmidt, 'Priority Steps to
Strengthen the Nonproliferation Regime',
Policy Outlook, Carnegie Endowment
for International Peace, no. 33, February
2007, http://www.carnegieendowment.
org/files/goldschmidt_priority_steps_
final.pdf.

24 *Ibid.*

Chapter Three

1 The introduction to this chapter is adapted
from Dana H. Allin, 'The Atlantic Crisis
of Confidence', *International Affairs*, vol.
80, no. 4, July 2004, pp. 649–63.

2 Interview with Secretary of State
Madeleine Albright, *Today*, NBC, 19
February 1998. This was not just an
American sentiment. Then-leader of the
German Green Party Joschka Fischer
argued in strikingly similar terms that the
US role was crucial in bringing peace to
Bosnia.

3 2002 *National Security Strategy of the United
States of America*; Council of the European
Union, 'A Secure Europe in a Better World:
European Security Strategy', Brussels, 12
December 2003, available at http://ue.eu.
int/uedocs/cmsUpload/78367.pdf.

4 Robert Chase, Emily Hill and Paul
Kennedy (eds), *Pivotal States: A New
Framework for U.S. Policy in the Developing
World* (New York: W.W. Norton, 2000).

5 Philip Gordon, Dana Allin and Phillip C.
Saunders, 'Iraq's Impact on the Future of
U.S. Foreign and Defense Policy, Session
2: The United States, Europe, and Asia',
Council on Foreign Relations, New York,
6 October 2006, transcript of discussion
at http://www.cfr.org/publication/11673/
iraqs_impact_on_the_future_of_us_
foreign_and_defense_policy.html?bread-
crumb=%2Fmedia%2Ftranscripts
%3Fpage%3D6.

6 Toby Dodge, 'The Causes of US Failure in
Iraq', *Survival*, no. 49, no. 1, Spring 2007,
p. 101.

7 Peter Beinart, 'War Torn', *The New
Republic*, 30 October 2006, p. 6.

8 Peter W. Galbraith and Reuel Marc
Gerecht, 'Should Iraq Be Partitioned?',
The New Republic Online, 4 November
2006. See also Jacob Weisberg, 'The War
That Dare Not Speak Its Name', *Financial
Times*, 28 September 2006, p. 19 for a
brief discussion of Gelb's and Galbraith's
proposals.

9 Dodge, 'The Causes of US Failure in
Iraq'.

10 Fareed Zakaria, 'Rethinking Iraq: The
Way Forward', *Newsweek*, 6 November
2006, p. 26.

11 *Ibid.* A similar plan was put forward by
Daniel Byman some 18 months earlier:
see Byman's 'Five Bad Options for Iraq',
Survival, vol. 47, no. 1, Spring 2005, pp.
7–32.

12 Steven N. Simon, *After the Surge: The
Case for U.S. Military Disengagement from
Iraq*, Council Special Report No. 23 (New
York: Council on Foreign Relations Press,
February 2007), p. 11.

13 James F. Dobbins et al., *America's Role
in Nation-Building: From Germany to Iraq*
(Santa Monica, CA: RAND, 2003), pp.
167–221.

14 Allin and Simon, 'Military Force Will
Not Defeat Islamist Revivalism', *Financial
Times*, 10 October 2006, p. 11.

15 The Iranians have been arming Shia
militias and, it has even been suggested,
Sunni insurgents, with the clear intention of making America's difficulties as

pronounced as possible. US–Iranian antagonism is a fact of life that will continue to be played out in Iraq. But the Iranians have cross-cutting interests in a stable and friendly Iraqi government; this interest that they share with the United States will become more evident as an American departure comes closer. Indeed, on the occasion of the first US–Iranian talks, Iran's deputy foreign minister, Abbas Araghchi, told the *Financial Times* that, although Iran does want US troops to leave, 'immediate withdrawal could lead to chaos, civil war. No one is asking for immediate withdrawal of foreign forces from Iraq.' Gareth Smyth, 'Iran Offers to Help US Find Iraq Exit', *Financial Times*, 9 May 2007, p. 10.

[16] See Tony Blair, 'PM's World Affairs Speech to the Lord Mayor's Banquet', 13 November 2006, http://www.number10.gov.uk/output/Page10409.asp.

[17] The Iraq Study Group Report, http://bakerinstitute.org/Pubs/iraqstudygroup_findings.pdf pp. 34–6.

[18] The administration's attitude was illustrated by President Bush's endorsement of 14 reservations by the Israeli government to the initial roadmap, and his later interpretation of two key final-status issues, borders and refugees, which acknowledged 'new realities on the ground', in a letter to Ariel Sharon, George W. Bush, 'Letter From President Bush to Prime Minister Sharon', 14 April 2004, http://www.whitehouse.gov/news/releases/2004/04/20040414-3.html.

[19] Which previous schemes, such as the Tenet plan, had included.

[20] Yezid Sayigh, 'Inducing a Failed State in Palestine', *Survival*, vol. 49, no. 3, Autumn 2007, pp. 14–15.

[21] On 15 July 2007, President Bush pledged $190 million in direct aid to the Fatah government to be transferred by the end of September, and announced an international conference for that autumn to review progress on building Palestinian institutions. The conference would be presided over by Condoleezza Rice and would include Israel, the Palestinian Authority and regional Arab states.

[22] Doug Suisman, Steven Simon, Glenn Robinson, C. Ross Anthony and Michael Schoenbaum, *The Arc: A Formal Structure for a Palestinian State* (Santa Monica, CA: RAND, 2007), available at http://www.rand.org/pubs/monographs/MG327-1/.

[23] Seth G. Jones, 'Averting Failure in Afghanistan', *Survival*, vol. 48, no. 1, Spring 2006, p. 115.

[24] James Dobbins' team at the RAND Corporation has argued that such operations require a ratio of 20 security personnel (both military and police included) to 1,000 people.

[25] Barnett R. Rubin, 'Saving Afghanistan', *Foreign Affairs*, vol. 86, no. 1, January–February 2007, p. 58.

[26] *Ibid.*, p. 71.

[27] Jones, 'Pakistan's Dangerous Game', *Survival*, vol. 49, no. 1, Spring 2007, pp. 15–32.

[28] Ian Bremmer, *The J Curve: A New Way to Understand Why Nations Rise and Fall* (New York: Simon and Schuster, 2006), p. 41.

[29] *Ibid.*, pp. 31–2.

[30] Dobbins, 'America's Role in Nation-building: From Germany to Iraq', *Survival*, vol. 45, no. 4, Winter 2003–04, pp. 87–110.

[31] Leo Tindemans et al., *Unfinished Peace: Report of the International Commission on the Balkans* (Washington DC: Carnegie Endowment for International Peace, 1996). Dana Allin was a co-author of this report.

[32] Report of the Secretary-General pursuant to General Assembly Resolution: The Fall of Srebrenica, A/54/549 (New York: United Nations, 1999), paragraphs 497–502, available at http://www.un.org/News/ossg/srebrenica.pdf.

[33] Dobbins, 'The UN's Role in Nation-building: From the Belgian Congo to Iraq', *Survival*, vol. 46, no. 4, Winter 2004–05, pp. 81–102.

[34] *Ibid.*, p. 98.

[35] Beinart, 'Blue Crush', *The New Republic*, 11 December 2006, p. 6.

36 See http://europa.eu.int/council/off/ conclu/dec99/dec99_en.htm#security

37 Bastian Giegerich and William Wallace, 'Not Such a Soft Power', *Survival*, vol. 46, no. 2, Summer 2004, pp. 163–82.

38 See Tony Blair, 'Doctrine of the International Community', speech delivered to the Economic Club, Chicago, 24 April 1999, http://www.pm.gov.uk/ output/Page1297.asp; and 'Address at the Labour Party Conference', 2 October 2001, http://www.americanrhetoric.com/ speeches/tblair10-02-01.htm.

39 Morton Abramowitz, 'After Iraq, Shrinking Horizons', *The Washington Post*, 31 July 2003, p. A19.

40 Dobbins, 'America's Role in Nation-building: From Germany to Iraq', p. 109.

41 Shibley Telhami, 'America in Arab Eyes', *Survival*, vol. 49, no. 1, Spring 2007, p. 114.

Conclusion

1 In effect, a combination of global US leadership with formal deference to the UN, the views of allies, and multilateral norms and institutions.

2 Lawrence Freedman, 'The Transatlantic Agenda: Vision and Counter-Vision', *Survival*, vol. 47, no. 4, Winter 2005–06, pp. 21, 23. Freedman cites Weber's two ethics from Max Weber, 'Politics as a Vocation', in H.H. Garth and C. Wright Mills (eds), *Essays in Sociology* (New York: Macmillan, 1946), pp. 26–45.

3 *Ibid.*, p. 23.

4 *Ibid.*, p. 36.

5 Allin, 'American Power and Allied Restraint: Lessons of Iraq', *Survival*, vol. 49, no. 1, Spring 2007, pp. 123–40.

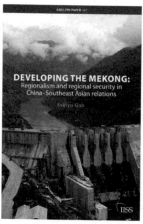
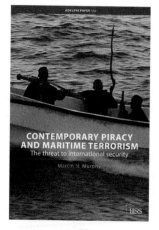